CIRLA'S STORY

CIRLA LEWIS

To Ben
with all good wishes
Cirla Lewis

MINERVA PRESS
MONTREUX LONDON WASHINGTON

Cirla L@nsa.com

ISBN 1 85863 570 5

First Published 1995 by
MINERVA PRESS
195 Knightsbridge
London SW7 1RE

2nd Impression 1996
3rd Impression 1997
4th Impression 1998

Printed in Great Britain for Minerva Press

CIRLA'S STORY

In memory of my Mother and Father.

To my dear husband, Phillip, for his support and encouragement.

My beloved Mother and dear Aunt Yetta talked about the past - and I listened.
Without them, this book would not have been written.

The author

Acknowledgement

The writer wishes to record her appreciation to Martin Gilbert, the historian, for his celebrated work on the 'Second World War', published by Weidenfeld and Nicolson, London, 1989. Extracts from this work appear in the Appendix, together with some additional material provided by Cirla Lewis.

Contents

Foreword

This true story is told so that my son and his generation will not forget the suffering and the courage of those people who lived through the Second World War.

I believe it is fitting for me to repeat the words from our Memorial Service, read every year on Yom Kippur, in our synagogue.

"We remember our six million dead and all who died when evil ruled the world. We remember those we knew and those whose very names are lost.

"We mourn for all that died with them; their goodness and their wisdom, which could have saved the world and healed so many wounds. We mourn for the genius and the wit that died, the learning and the laughter that were lost. The world has become a poorer place, and our hearts grow cold as we think of the splendour that might have been.

"We stand in gratitude for their example of decency and goodness. They are like candles which shine out from the darkness of those years, and in their light we know what goodness is - and evil.

"We salute those men and women who were not Jews, who had the courage to stand outside the mob and suffer with us. They, too, are Your witnesses, a source of hope when we despair."

We remember:

Auschwitz

Lodz

Ponar

Babi Yar

Maidanek

Birkenau

Kovno

Janowska

Theresienstadt

Buchenwald

Treblinka

Vilna

Bergen-Belsen

Mauthausen

Dachau

Minsk

Warsaw

For background interest to the reader, a list of some of the more important dates which occurred during the period of 'Cirla's Story' are given on page xiii.

These cover the period from the Munich Agreement between Chamberlain, Daladier, Hitler and Mussolini on September 29th 1938 to the German surrender in Berlin on May 8th 1945.

The geographical location of the principal places mentioned in the story are illustrated in the map on page xix.

An account of some of the principal events concerning the Second World War, which particularly related to Belgium, Holland and France from the conquest and occupation by Germany, through to the eventual liberation by the Allies is to be found in the appendix.

This is not to be viewed, in any way, as a comprehensive or complete record of these events but has been selected by the writer to be of particular relevance to 'Cirla's Story'.

A major reason for writing this account is to pay tribute to the enormous courage displayed by so many people, whether members of the Resistance Movement or just private individuals, who went out of their way, at considerable risk to themselves and their families, to help save the lives of those targeted for persecution by the Nazis.

The writer has submitted the names and personal details of members of her family, who perished in the Holocaust, to the Department for the Righteous at Yad Vashem, The Holocaust Martyrs' and Heroes' Remembrance Authority in Jerusalem, Israel.

The names of those who were instrumental in saving the writer from the clutches of the Nazis were passed on to Yad

Vashem, as one of the principal duties of this Authority is to convey the gratitude of the Jewish people to those non-Jews who risked their lives to save Jews during the Holocaust.

Betty Liem, Jean-Louis Liem and Marie Arekens were posthumously honoured as 'Righteous Gentiles' by Yad Vashem. Their names were engraved on the wall of 'The Righteous Among the Nations', at the Yad Vashem Memorial in Jerusalem.

Some Important Dates

September 29th 1938

Munich Agreement between Chamberlain, Daladier, Hitler and Mussolini.

April 27th 1939

Conscription introduced in Great Britain.

May 25th 1939

Anglo-Polish Treaty signed in London.

August 23rd 1939

German-Soviet Pact signed by von Ribbentrop.

September 1st 1939

Poland invaded by German Forces.

Great Britain and France mobilised.

September 6th 1939

First enemy air raid on Britain.

May 10th 1940

Holland, Belgium and Luxembourg invaded by German forces.

May 17th 1940

Belgian Government moved to Ostend.

May 27th 1940

Belgian army capitulated on the order of King Leopold.

May 27th - June 4th 1940

Evacuation of British troops from Dunkirk.

June 3rd 1940

German Air Force bombed Paris.

June 14th 1940

German military vehicles at the Place de la Concorde.

June 17th 1940

Marshal Pétain formed a new Government for France.

June 18th 1940

General De Gaulle broadcast from London to the French people.

June 20th 1940

French delegation travelled to Rethondes to negotiate Armistice.

September 15th 1940

Battle of Britain ended with British victory.

June 1942

Eichmann announced plan for deportation of Jews.

June 6th 1944

D-Day: invasion of Europe by the Allied forces.

September 3rd 1944

Allies in Belgium.

September 4th 1944

Antwerp and Brussels liberated from the Germans by the Allies.

October 13th 1944

Hitler commenced offensive on the Ardennes, Belgium.

October 13th 1944

Antwerp hit by German V2 rocket and V1 flying bomb.

April 29th 1945

Operation Manna took place.

May 5th 1945

Germans surrendered in Holland.

May 7th 1945

Signing of complete surrender at Reims.

May 8th 1945

Berlin - further signing of the German surrender took place.

List of Photographs

1   From left to right, Flore, Yetta, Babe, nursemaid and Soura Kriksman (ca 1913).

2   From left to right, Yetta, Flore and Babe (ca 1919).

3   Three young ladies - from left to right, Babe, Yetta and Flore (ca 1929).

4   Jacob (Jaap) Italiaander (ca 1930).

5   Flore and Jaap on their wedding day (1935).

6   Back row, from left to right: Henri, Madeleine and Oncle Jean; front row, from left to right: Suzy (Cirla), Flore, Tante Betty and Gilberte Liem (1944).

7   Back row, from left to right: a friend of the family, Tante Betty, Gilberte, Tom Young, a British soldier, M. Sendyk (a friend);
     Front row, from left to right: Flore, Oncle Jean, Henri's wife, Suzy wearing the British soldier's beret, Mme. Sendyk (a friend) and Madeleine - the Liberation (1944).

8   From left to right: Flore, Madeleine (in the foreground), Tom and one of the British soldiers who liberated Ghent. A bottle of champagne was dug up from the garden! (1944).

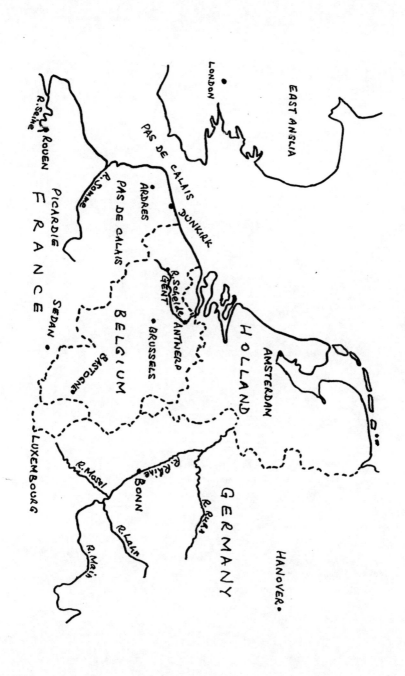

1 Mendel and Soura

Mendel Selmanoff Kriksman was born in Varka, on the 1st January 1872.

His father had a thriving wine merchant's business.

As was usual in Jewish families, his parents had been blessed with many children. He was the eldest son. At first he was quite a chubby child but as he grew up he became tall and lanky. He had an open face and when he smiled one could see strong regular white teeth. He knew they were strong because he often bent coins with them, when he was showing off to the other boys. They could sometimes beat him at arm wrestling but all were amazed and quite envious when he showed them his tour de force.

Up to the age of thirteen he had gone to the local school and also attended the synagogue's religious classes, where he was taught Hebrew and learned what it meant to be a Jew. Not that he wanted to be reminded of the fact too often.

This part of Poland was sometimes Polish and then at other times Russian. Not that it made any difference to the Jews who lived there. As a Jew you went about your business and tried not to be noticed.

When Mendel's father's business started to lose money and he feared that he would not be able to pass on a thriving concern to his eldest son, it was decided that it would be wiser for Mendel to learn a trade.

What could be better but for the boy to go as an apprentice at a goldsmith's in the nearby village? He would learn the trade, receive food and lodging and at certain times would be expected to help the goldsmith's wife with her chores.

Once vetted and accepted, Mendel would sit for hours, polishing gold rings, setting diamonds into intricate designs, under the watchful eye of his employer.

The customers were demanding but when the work was done Mendel felt a sense of achievement.

He had his dream - one day he would be free - free to live a life in a place where being a Jew did not mean that you had fear in your heart.

A previous day Mendel had been given a big tip by a satisfied customer. Mr. Mandelbaum was leaving to go to Belgium - this was the reason why he had so many pieces of expensive jewellery made. After all, he could not take his other belongings with him.

He would sell his house and those who bought it would get a bargain. They knew he wanted to leave Poland, so they would make a reasonable offer. No, they would not cheat him exactly, but they would, of course, not pay him the full value either.

Anyway, Mr. Mandelbaum was overjoyed - in this distant country he would be going to, he would be able to sell his jewellery and live on the proceeds, until he found himself some work. After all, a tailor should be able to make a living. His wife and children were also looking forward to their new life.

From time to time, Mendel was allowed to go home to his parents' house. How happy they were to see him. His father and mother would listen to his stories and were anxious to know whether he ate well and were the goldsmith and his wife kind to him?

Did he know that the shadchen (matchmaker) had come round to enquire after him?

Mendel's eyes blazed with anger. No! He wasn't interested! He would choose a wife one day and didn't need a matchmaker.

His parents looked at each other and wondered why the boy was so angry. Weren't they happily married? Theirs had been an arranged marriage. Well, they would just tell the shadchen that Mendel was still too young to think of marriage.

Mendel knew whom he wanted to marry but he decided to say nothing about it to his parents.

She was lovely. Her name was Soura Boroukharina Mendeleona.

He had seen her one day when she left the synagogue with her relatives. He had smiled at her and she had returned his smile. He closed his eyes and remembered. Yes, she had looked at him with her lovely blue eyes, fringed by dark lashes. Her pale face was framed by thick black hair. She was not very tall but she had a graceful slender body. He knew that this was the girl he would ask to become his wife one day.

Four years later, his apprenticeship came to an end.

Mendel had seen Soura at the synagogue on many occasions and he knew that she had not yet been promised in marriage to anyone.

One evening, he decided to speak to his parents. What! He had someone in mind - who was she? A suitable bride-to-be? Soura Pinkus - yes, they knew the family. Indeed, they were very well respected people and she would undoubtedly also bring with her a substantial dowry. They would not be able to approach her parents directly. It would have to be done through the shadchen.

Mendel felt he had better accept this procedure. He did so want the girl of his dreams!

A few weeks later, the two young people met at the home of the prospective bride. Mendel's and Soura's parents talked things over. Times were bad. Soura's dowry would be quite small.

Well, for the sake of their son's happiness, what did a dowry really matter - let the young couple be happy!

Mendel was on cloud nine. They would wait to get married. In two years - with his trade - they would be able to save enough money to start a life together. Luck was on his side.

A few days later, the postman delivered an official looking letter. It was addressed to Mendel.

There, for all to see, were his call-up papers. No, he did not want to join the army - but did he have any choice?

There was one way out of this dilemma. He could have one of his toes amputated - gruesome, but certainly effective. He knew that this was how some young men had managed to avoid conscription.

Soura and Mendel met. All the relatives were there as well.

No, the young people could not leave the country. In any case, if Mendel were to leave now, and went abroad he would never be able to come back. He would be classed as a deserter.

After long discussions and tears, there was only one conclusion they all came to - Mendel would join the army and Soura would wait for his return.

When Mendel returned to his home town, Soura was overjoyed. She had waited patiently and had written long letters to her fiancé. She had even managed to save up some money from all the beautiful needlework she had been able to do for neighbours and friends of the family.

Why wait any longer? The young couple had an orthodox wedding ceremony and a few days later they left Poland forever. They would spend their future life together in Belgium.

The years passed and Mendel became a successful diamond merchant. Their great sadness was that they did not have any children. Mendel took Soura to eminent physicians who were puzzled.

By Jewish law, Mendel had the right to ask for a religious divorce. Ten years was a long time to wait!

Then the miracle happened - Soura became pregnant. The first child was born. They called her Flore. Three years later, they were blessed with another little girl - they named her Estera - later she would be known as Yetta.

As Mendel had become a wealthy man, he could afford to keep his wife and children in luxury. Soura had a maid to do all the household chores. Life was good and theirs was a happy household.

Then one day, Soura told her little daughters that another baby was on the way. Would it be a boy or a girl? To the great delight of Flore and Yetta, the new addition to the family was female. When the Rabbi visited, he was told that they wanted to call the child Berthe - was there a Jewish equivalent?

As the girls grew into adolescence, there was no doubt in everyone's mind that they would blossom into lovely young women. The shadchen would have no trouble at all in finding suitable husbands for them.

2 Mauritz and Rachel

Born towards the end of the nineteenth century; Mauritz Italiaander had not had an easy childhood. His mother, a widow, had put him into an orphanage where it was discovered that the boy had a talent for drawing.

When one of the benefactors came to look round the orphanage, Mauritz was introduced to the middle-aged man, who decided that he would pay for the boy's training at one of the art schools in Amsterdam.

Mauritz worked terribly hard and, when he finally obtained his diploma, established himself in the Jewish quarter of Amsterdam.

Mauritz and his wife, Rachel, loved the Weesperstraat. They felt at home amongst their Jewish friends. From morning till night the street was bustling. The food shops were full of people buying Jewish and Dutch fare.

Friends would climb the steep stairs to visit the young couple. The apartment was divided into living quarters on one floor and the room at the top of the building was light and airy. This was where Mauritz did all his painting.

When friends came round, Rachel would always offer them coffee and some homebaked boterkoek (a very moist cake made from flour, sugar and a great deal of butter).

Mauritz was a handsome man. His thick black hair was rather unruly. His grey eyes seemed to smile at the world and, although he was not very tall, he commanded respect from those around him.

Mauritz was happiest in his studio where he would spend hours on end perfecting a scene depicting high gabled Dutch houses overlooking the picturesque Amsterdam canals.

Like all artists, Mauritz was not easy to live with.

When things did not go well with his painting, he would leave his studio and come down to the living room - look around and complain in a loud voice about the dust on the furniture.

When times were good and Mauritz sold many paintings, Rachel would engage a maid to do the cleaning. Invariably, servants would not stay long in the household.

Rachel was quite often irritated by her husband and their relationship was, at times, somewhat volatile.

When she sulked, Mauritz would go up to her and coax her to sit for him. He would take out a pad and in no time would sketch a portrait of his young wife. With her long blond hair down to her waist, big blue eyes, oval face, her full lips were meant to be kissed. He was indeed a lucky man.

Most people forgave Mauritz his eccentric behaviour. After all, he was an artist and artists didn't have to conform to the normal expectations of polite society.

Then there were the occasions when Rachel and Mauritz would go out together and he would stop in the street, point to a complete stranger and comment on the physique of the person. What a profile, what interesting bone structure!

After a few years of married life, Rachel became pregnant. It was a bouncing boy. They named him Jacob. As he grew up, his Dutch friends called him Jaap.

A year later, a daughter, Lien, was born. She was a small baby and needed a great deal of attention.

Jaap was a happy child. He would often sit in his father's studio and watch Mauritz paint.

Wherever Jaap went, people remarked on his sturdy physique. The boy had a high forehead, thick light auburn hair and grey eyes which looked straight at you. He enjoyed life to the full. Often, when he was given pocket money, he spent it immediately. When he was broke, he would go to his sister, Lien, who would admonish him for being such a spendthrift.

As he reached his early twenties, his anxious parents looked on and urged him to think of the future.

At school, he had excelled in languages and Mauritz suggested to his son that he could perhaps go to Paris to improve his French and could take a few paintings with him to sell.

Jaap left Amsterdam full of enthusiasm and arrived in Paris thinking of all the wonderful things he could do in this exciting city.

The boulevards and cafés looked so inviting. Jaap managed to sell quite a number of his father's paintings. Somehow, life was there to be enjoyed and when the time came to send some money home to his father, very little seemed to be left.

Jaap had to return to Amsterdam when the money ran out. His French was fluent and he had acquired an air of sophistication. Mauritz, however, was not too thrilled at the prospect of his son going from one job to another.

Jaap then went to Germany, to perfect his German. Once again, he frittered away all the proceeds of the sale of the paintings.

When he finally came back to Holland, it was time to take stock of his achievements. He had had a splendid time but what did he have to show for it?

Amsterdam felt claustrophobic. He could no longer live with his parents. He would try to make a success of himself by going to Belgium. This time his father gave him some money and no paintings to sell. Mauritz had learned his lesson.

Jaap arrived in Antwerp, where his mother's cousin had settled.

Elie was a diamond cleaver. Elie was thick-set, had small pale eyes and was rapidly becoming bald. Nevertheless, women seemed to like him or was it his money they liked most of all?

He had married against the wishes of his parents. His wife was a pretty woman with rosy cheeks and big blue eyes. She adored her husband, although he was often unfaithful to her.

Elie remembered the scene well. When he told his father that the girl he had married was Catholic, the old man had remained silent for a minute or so. Then he looked at his son and uttered a cry of anguish. He, a Hebrew scholar - how could his son have done such a thing! Tears streamed down his face. He tore his jacket and Elie heard his father recite kaddish, the Hebrew prayer for the dead. Elie would never see his father again!

Jaap was made welcome by Elie and his wife, Nie. Of course, he could stay with them as long as he needed - until he found a permanent home for himself.

Life was hard at first. Jaap had several jobs as a salesman but what he really wanted was to start his own business. He knew exactly the field he wanted to go into. The one big problem was where could he find the capital?

A chance meeting with an old acquaintance from Amsterdam changed his life completely.

Vanhemde was a wealthy man. He was much older than Jaap and was quite willing to invest some money in a new venture. What did Jaap have in mind? Film distributing to cinemas. Well, if Jaap could make some calculations, he would be willing to become a sleeping partner.

A few weeks later, Jaap was in business. What a happy feeling. Mauritz and Rachel received long letters in which their son described his good fortune.

Jaap worked long hours and would return to his relatives' flat utterly exhausted.

One day, Nie suggested that he should try to make some time for relaxation. What about a Sunday afternoon? Why not go to a tea dance, to that lovely big hotel in town?

Well, why not! As he looked around and tried to find a table, he saw her. She was sitting with three other girls and a middle-aged lady, at a table near the dance floor.

As the music started to play, he walked over to the young girl and asked whether she would care to dance. She was tall and, when he looked at her face, he saw dark brown eyes, a straight nose, a well-shaped mouth and, as she smiled, he noticed that her teeth were brilliantly white. She had thick black hair and held her head high. He was curious to know who the middle-aged lady was. Was she here with her mother? Oh, no! That was Maman Arekens; she was their chaperone. She was a friend of the family and lived next door. She was accompanying her daughter, Thylla, and Flore's sisters.

Now he knew. Her name was Flore, Flore Kriksman. A foreign name. Jewish perhaps? He wondered whether they could meet again. Yes, she usually came to the tea dance at this hotel on Sundays. Perhaps next Sunday, if he was in town. Then it was time to say goodbye and she was gone.

As Jaap went home, he seemed to walk on air. What a splendid afternoon he had had! What a captivating girl!

As the week progressed, Jaap seemed to have more and more work piling up. I suppose he would have to work the week-end. Would Flore be at the tea dance? He would never know.

A few weeks later, he went back to the hotel. The band was playing a tango. There she was. He asked her to dance and she seemed rather cool. Could she forgive him? He had wanted to come but work had prevented him. How stupid of him! He had not even introduced himself! Jaap Italiaander was his name. He came from Amsterdam and he, too, was of the Jewish faith.

Jaap decided that he had wasted too much time. He would ask her whether she would accompany him to the cinema next Sunday. She accepted his invitation. He would be very welcome to come and have a cup of tea with her family before going out.

When Flore came home, Soura, her mother, wanted to know whether she had had a pleasant afternoon. What! She had met a charming man? Was he Jewish? Was he a professional man? She did not want her daughter to waste her time on a schlemiel (a dimwit).

That week-end, Jaap dressed with great care. He wanted to make a good impression on the Kriksman family.

As he was shown into the vast high-ceilinged drawing room, he handed a big bouquet of flowers to the maid. He sat down in a comfortable dark green velvet-covered armchair. The beautiful crystal chandelier sparkled like diamonds. There was also a long settee against one wall - against another stood a big glass cabinet which held some exquisite silverware. In the corner, he saw a piano. A musical family, undoubtedly.

He stood up as Flore and her sisters came in. She was the tallest and the eldest.

Yetta was the middle one. Although quite short, she had a pleasant face. Blue-grey eyes looked at him from behind glasses. Her light brown hair was cut short into a fashionable bob. She spoke in a relaxed manner.

The youngest sister was called Berthe but everyone knew her as 'Babe'. She was not very tall but somehow her features reminded him of Flore, although her eyes were blue.

Their mother came in last. She was middle-aged and he could see that she, too, had been quite beautiful, when young.

Tea was served and the conversation was quite animated. Did he like Belgium? Was he living with relatives? How strange that he had never learned Yiddish. He could see that Flore liked being with her family. Would he stay for supper?

Weeks passed and Jaap felt very much at home at the Kriksmans'.

He had even started to speak a little Yiddish which, needless to say, endeared him to Soura.

He knew that Flore was the girl he wanted to marry but somehow felt a certain unease. He had not yet met her father. He knew that her parents would have preferred an East European Jew as a son-in-law. Dutch Jews were considered to be far too integrated. He had seen the look of disbelief on

Soura's face when he had said that he did not speak Yiddish. What sort of a Jew was he? A good Jew but also a first class Dutchman!

As they walked in the garden one day, he looked at Flore and simply said that he loved her. Did she feel the same about him?

Of course she did! She had wondered how long it would take for him to declare himself.

Soura had told Mendel all about Jaap. Well, he would meet the young man and ask him a few searching questions. Would he be able to support his young wife? Would he see to it that they kept a Jewish home? Where would they live - hopefully not too far away, so that his daughter would still be able to visit her parents regularly?

Jaap was deliriously happy when his father-in-law to-be told him that he welcomed him into the family. Yes, he hoped he would be gaining a son.

It was the custom in Jewish orthodox families not to have long engagements. Everyone agreed that this made sense. After all, it was foolish to expect the young people to control their urges for too long. The wedding would take place in their home. It was to be an intimate affair; just the close family and a few dear friends.

Soura knew of an excellent cook, Gietele. So many of the Jewish ladies had employed her for their functions. God knows, that most of them were not easy to please. So, she would engage her to prepare all the food for the wedding feast. There had to be fish - maybe some poached halibut - followed by roast chicken, a selection of vegetables, latkes (potato pancakes) and dessert. It would have to be sorbets and fresh fruit salad; naturally, it was a kosher meal - what else!

The rabbi was delighted to hear the good news. Yes, he was willing to perform the religious ceremony in their home.

Everything looked perfect on the big day. The table in the dining room was set with the finest china. The silver cutlery

(left to right) Flore, Yetta, Babe, nursemaid and Soura Kirksman
(c. 1913)

(left to right) Yetta, Flore and Babe (c. 1919)

Three young ladies - from left to right, Babe, Yetta and Flore (c. 1929)

Jacob (Jaap) Italiaander (c.1930)

and exquisite vases filled with spring flowers looked so appealing.

The chupah (the marriage canopy) was standing in the drawing room.

The bride wore a long white velvet dress. Her veil was attached to a charming cap which fitted snugly onto her black hair. She wore no jewellery. She looked radiant.

Jaap looked most handsome in his dinner jacket. His hair, like all fashionable young men, had been sleekly combed back and smoothed down with haircream.

Yetta, in a pale green dress which had embroidery round the neckline, had taken off her spectacles to please her sister Flore. She asked herself whether she would one day meet someone with whom she would want to spend the rest of her life.

Babe, the youngest of the Kriksman daughters, looked quite adorable in her pink chiffon dress. She was going to be the next one to stand under the chupah in a few months' time. Her fiancé looked down at her. What a delightful girl! He was fortunate to have met her. Unbelievable, to think that he, too, was going to marry into the family - he, just like Jaap was Dutch and of the Jewish faith.

Lien, Jaap's sister, petite, blond and wearing a powder blue chiffon dress, which matched her eyes, was standing near the chupah holding onto the arm of her husband, Edu. They had recently come back from their honeymoon.

Mauritz had taken time off from his painting. Amsterdam seemed to be far away. He and Rachel stood with Flore's parents under the chupah. They looked at the young couple lovingly. What a happy day this was!

After the exchange of vows, the groom was asked to break a glass under his feet. All the guests then raised their voices in unison and the traditional mazeltov (good luck) filled the room.

Jaap and Flore were now man and wife.

3 From Antwerp to Dunkirk

I was born in 1935. I had a very happy childhood. My maternal grandmother - I called her Bonnemama - would visit us every day. I would listen to her as she spoke to my mother in Yiddish. "Did the child sleep well? What did you give her for breakfast? What! She only wanted a banana - no wonder she is so thin. Come to me for lunch; I'll give Cirlake* some fried chicken livers - that's what she likes!"

As she sat down in an armchair, I looked at her shiny face. She wore no make-up and her grey hair was pulled back into a bun. Her lively blue eyes would look around and she would shake her head and ask, "Floreke, where is Marie?" Marie was Mama's cleaning lady. "So, you have not finished the housework? Oy, the child needs fresh air; I'll take her to the park. I'll be sitting on my usual bench, you know the one, near the entrance."

When I looked up at Mama, she smiled at me and just said, "Come Cirlake, put on your coat and be a good girl with your Bonnemama."

Mama was the eldest daughter. She was tall - her hair was jet black and when she looked at me, her child, she smiled, as if to say you are my greatest treasure. She didn't, of course, always smile. No, I remembered quite vividly how her face had turned quite red when she discovered the empty box of chocolates. I had dragged a stool near the mantelpiece in Mama's bedroom and climbed on it. How clever of me; now I could reach the box. I had very generously shared the chocolates with my cousin, Danielle, who came to tea that afternoon. We finished the entire contents between us! How

---

* In Dutch, the suffix 'ke' denotes endearment and one could say that it means 'little'. It is used in Belgium and Holland. Hence, 'Cirla' becomes 'Cirlake'.

was I to know that laxatives were special chocolates that gave children a tummy ache?

After our walk in the park, we would go to Bonnemama's for lunch. My grandparents lived in a big house. I particularly loved to sit in the vast living room with its high ceiling, crystal chandelier and armchairs covered with dark green velvet. How I admired the cabinet in which Bonnemama kept all her silver - even silver glass holders which were used when we drank lemon tea after meals.

At about two o'clock in the afternoon, my grandfather would come home from the Diamond Bourse. He was a diamond merchant and had come to Antwerp many years ago, with his then young wife. Life in Poland had been hard for them both. Who in his right mind would want to stay in a country where pogroms were rife? Here, in Belgium, one was free to live a decent life.

After lunch, Bonpapa would sit down in his armchair. Tommy, the Alsatian dog, would be allowed in and I would climb up onto my grandfather's knee. Then it was story time. "Cirlake, do you want to listen to the story of baby Moses?" he would ask. I would look up into his thin face and nod. At times, I would pull at his grey moustache and then he would frown and put me on a stool beside him.

Quite often, Bonpapa would not go back to the Diamond Bourse but stay and listen to Mama play the piano. When Mama had finished, I would climb up onto the piano bench and ask, "Can I play my tune?" Everyone was delighted with my rendering of "Frère Jacques, frère Jacques, dormez vous?" Bonnemama would say, "This child has talent. Who knows, Floreke, she may be a better pianist than you one day."

Then it was time to go home. "Come, Cirlake, get into your pushchair. We mustn't be late for Papa."

I knew Papa worked in Brussels. He owned a company distributing films to cinemas. He owned the films and would hire them out. How I liked going with both my parents to see Shirley Temple dance and sing in the cinema in town. That was a week-end treat.

Invariably, Papa was home late - a last minute client to deal with or mail to be signed.

I would wait up in my nightdress and listen for the noise of the key turning in the keyhole. There he stood, a fine looking man, only as tall as Mama. His shiny light auburn hair was neatly combed. His grey eyes smiled at me. "Well, Cirlake, how is my little girl - have you been good today?" I would rush into his arms and he would carry me to bed. After having had dinner, he would come into my room and, if I wasn't asleep, he would sit down next to my bed and read me a story. The story would invariably be in Dutch. It was understood that I should learn his mother tongue. He was a Jew but born in Holland and he felt proud to be a Dutchman.

As I closed my eyes, I knew I was greatly loved.

One morning, I woke up to be told, "Cirlake, Opa and Oma* are coming from Amsterdam. They will be staying with us for a few days."

What excitement - Opa was such fun! He was a landscape painter by profession. If anyone looked the part, he certainly did. He was a handsome man with a shock of thick white hair. Although not very tall, he commanded respect from those around him. In the Weesperstraat, which was a bustling Jewish neighbourhood - where my paternal grandparents lived - Opa was known as 'our famous painter'. His Dutch landscapes were recognised as 'an Italiaander'. When times were bad, he even did a few Frans Hals copies, to keep the bailiffs from the door. He never signed them. The man who sold them for him explained to the buyers - a great many Americans - "These are unsigned. You do know Frans Hals, don't you? It's not the

---

* In Dutch, the words 'Opa' and 'Oma' mean grandfather and grandmother, respectively.

genuine article but a very good copy." Needless to say, some
went back with the new owners, who may have told their
friends, "Hey, what do you think of my Frans Hals? Picked it
up in Amsterdam!"

Mama would be very busy; cooking and baking. I was told,
"Cirlake, do some nice drawings for Opa." When they arrived,
tired, thirsty and hungry from the long journey, they would
embrace me and hug me and say, "Cirlake, you've grown since
we last saw you. What! Some more drawings?" Opa would
put on his glasses and give a knowing smile. He would
comment, "Of course, I can see that the child takes after me.
Encouragement, that's what the child needs, ja, ja."

Oma was blond and had blue eyes. People would say, "She
is petite for a Dutch woman." She loved getting dressed and
going out in the afternoons to have tea and pastries in the
patisseries in town.

At times, Mama looked harassed and when Papa came home
in the evening and Oma would go on about what a lovely day
she had had, Mama looked positively angry.

At the end of the week, when it was time for Oma and Opa
to go back to Amsterdam, everyone was smiling again - I
wondered why.

After they had gone, we went back to the same old routine.

And then it happened. I overheard Mama and Papa talking.
"Jaap, what are we going to do?" Papa tried to calm down
Mama. "Floreke, don't worry so much. This Hitler fellow is
just a big mouth." I wondered who this man Hitler was. All
the adults around me looked concerned and people no longer
smiled so readily.

Bonnemama and Bonpapa looked sad. I listened very
carefully to the conversation of the grown-ups. "No, Floreke,
we are not leaving our home," said Bonnemama. What did it
all mean?

A few days later, we went to say goodbye to my
grandparents. With tears in their eyes, they hugged me and

said, "Cirlake, you are going on a long trip. Be obedient and listen to your Mama and Papa."

When we got back to the flat, Mama packed the suitcases hurriedly. Just the essentials - this wasn't a holiday trip. As we left our home, I wondered why I hadn't been allowed to take more toys with me. Mama had said, "Choose your favourite doll, Cirlake." I had started to cry and could see that, if I didn't stop stamping my feet, Papa would give my bottom a good roasting!

The station was not too far away. I was looking forward to a long train journey.

As I held Papa's hand, I saw people rushing past us. They seemed to be panic-stricken. An elderly man spoke to us, "War has been declared; the Boches have taken Poland."

At the station, men, women and children were boarding trains. The French coast was the destination and then, hopefully, a ship to England.

I looked around me and it didn't seem as if this trip was going to be much fun. I sat on Mama's knees and listened to all the passengers talking. There was mention of that nasty man Hitler again. Then, after about an hour, the speeding train stopped in the middle of the countryside. Some of the passengers opened the windows; what was going on? Before anyone could move, we heard planes overhead. The noise was deafening. The train shook and the doors flew open. Papa yelled, "Floreke, jump!" and I was dragged along in the mêlée. People screamed, "We're being bombed!" We ran as fast as we could. We just kept going - we didn't look back.

When we emerged from the ditch in which we had thrown ourselves, Papa kissed me and said, "Come, Cirlake, have a ride on my shoulders."

It was a hot sunny day. Men, women and children carried what they managed to salvage of their belongings. Papa was holding one small suitcase and Mama the other. Then we saw it - an old pram - wonderful; our suitcases could be put in it and Mama said, "You, Cirlake, can sit on top."

From time to time, the planes came back. Everyone jumped into the ditches as one explosion after the other shook the earth beneath our feet. As we marched on, I couldn't understand why some people were just lying there. Why didn't they get up?

People just walked on wearily - as if they hoped to reach a safe haven at the end of the journey.

We came to a bend in the road and Mama stopped and waved her arms in the air. "Jaap, can you see, over there - Yetta, Cissie, Aaron and Reggie?"

A slender young woman came towards us. She had a small suitcase with her. She ran towards my mother, "Oh, Floreke, how wonderful to see you! Are you trying to make it to the coast?" There she was, my favourite aunt. We would all stay together. Cissie, a small nervous-looking woman, smiled, shook her head and said, "This is a miracle." Her husband, a big tall sturdy fellow, slapped Papa on the back. I remembered that they had visited Bonnemama one afternoon and she had said, "Shake hands, Cirlake. This is my friend Cissie, and her husband Aaron."

Reggie was Bonnemama's cousin. She didn't look at all like a relative. She had a huge face, beady eyes, a rather long nose and a freckled skin. As I gazed down at her, from where I sat on top of all the suitcases, it occurred to me that she could be the bad witch from one of the fairy tales I so enjoyed listening to. She joined our party and we continued our journey.

A Citroen car, hooter going full blast, drove past us. A grey-haired man looked out of the side window. "Hey, Jaap! Over here!" he called out. Papa rushed towards the car and, from where I sat, I heard him say, "Vanhemde, you devil! How did you manage to get this car?" The man, his companion and a teenager sitting in the back seat, all laughed. "Money, money, that's all you need, Jaap, my boy!" came the reply.

"Where are you heading?" asked Vanhemde. He, too, was going to try to get to England - far away from the Boches.

40

Vanhemde looked at our group and said, "Come on, Jaap, I can take three people. Hop in."

I saw Mama talk to Papa. How could we leave the rest of them behind? No, we would stay together and manage somehow to get to our destination.

"Well, can't hang about - see you in London!" shouted Vanhemde and off he went.

Our group trudged on. The sun was setting. "We must find a place to rest," said Papa. And there it was - a farmhouse - only a few more yards to go. We approached cautiously. We had just seen a road sign - Ardres - it was somewhere in France, at least!

The door was ajar. It was quite dark inside. Before anyone could find the light switch, a ghostlike figure came forward. She was holding a candlestick in her right hand. The light flickered. She was a woman in her early thirties. Dark brown straight hair framed a bronzed face. Her flashing eyes looked angrily at us. Then she spoke, "Vous parlez le français?" Mama went up to her and smiled, "Oui, madame. Êtes-vous la propriétaire de cette ferme?" No, she wasn't the proprietor of the farm. Just like us, she, too, was trying to get away as far as possible from the Germans. She was taking refuge in this place with her mother and young son. Her husband was a major in the French army. She didn't know where he was right now.

We made ourselves comfortable and shared some food we found in the larder with our new-found friends.

A few days passed by. I liked it on the farm although there didn't seem to be many animals left - a few sheep and two ginger cats. When I stroked the cats, all the grown-ups kept on saying, "Cirlake, mind you don't get scratched." Why should the cats scratch me? They were my friends.

One afternoon, the silence was broken. As we looked out of the window, we saw some heavy army vehicles coming towards us. Mama and everyone in the room looked agitated.

The young French woman, who shared the farm with us, went to the door and opened it.

Five German officers got out of their Mercedes car.

They walked towards the farm. When they reached the door, we could hear them say, "Good afternoon, madame. We would like to come in. We have had a very tiring journey." Then, one of the officers called to a soldier, "Hey, you! Come here! Go into the cellar and see if there is any wine or champagne. We shall have a drink with these good people."

Although I was only five years old, I didn't think it was very polite of him to come and order us about.

When the bottles were brought, the soldier filled the glasses and everyone was given one. We, the children, were just ignored.

"This looks like good champagne," said one of the Germans.

"Now let us drink to the Führer. Heil Hitler!"

Madame Delfarge, the French woman, took the glass, looked at the Germans and said in a voice shaking with anger, "No, I do not drink with the Boches," and threw her glass onto the floor. None of us moved. We heard voices and shouting in the yard and the door flew open. "Forgive me, Herr Major - headquarters. They wish us to move on," said a breathless young soldier. The Germans put their glasses down on the table and did not say another word. They clicked their heels and left.

Madame Delfarge turned towards us and screamed, "How could you all just stand there? Why did you not say anything?"

Mama spoke very quietly, "We are Jews, madame." The young woman answered, "I had no idea - I apologise."

Everyone in the room breathed a sigh of relief. Who knows what we had escaped?

It was time for us to move on. We had to get to the coast!

At last, here we were in Dunkirk. I looked around me and saw people running everywhere.

"Let's go to the docks," said Papa. It all looked so chaotic. Small boats were taking British soldiers on board and army and navy types were yelling at the top of their voices.

"Come on, we haven't got all day. Get a move on!"

Mama, who could speak English very well - she had been brought up in England during the First World War - went to speak to one of the officers in charge.

"I am sorry to trouble you, Captain. We are desperate. Can you help us? We want to get to England. Please take us with you." He looked at Mama and answered,

"Dear lady, I would if I could but my orders are - army and navy personnel only. I am so sorry."

What was going to happen? Papa said in a decisive voice, "Well, it's no use. We must take a decision. Do you agree with me that we should try to find a place to spend the night?" Our little group went back into the town. We would try to find a few rooms in one of the hotels. Wherever we went, we were told, "No, we have no vacancies. Try around the corner." By now, darkness had set in. As we shuffled down the road, we could see a vast building a few hundred yards away. There it was - a convent; perhaps we could find shelter within its walls.

The door was opened by a young nun. Mama spoke to her; "Good evening, Sister. We have nowhere to go. Can you give us shelter for the night?" She told us that there were already many people inside. She hesitated. Then she saw me. "Come in, we shall manage somehow," she said. Tables were turned upside down and a few mattresses appeared. I liked my new bed. It was quite comfortable too.

As I closed my eyes, I heard the noise of planes overhead. It felt as if the earth was shaking. Dunkirk was being bombarded - by the Germans or the British - nobody knew nor cared.

From the chapel came heavenly music as the nuns were singing their prayers. I wondered whether God could hear them.

In the morning, the grown-ups were given hot coffee. For the children, there was hot chocolate. The croissants baked by some of the nuns were delicious.

Sister Superior came to see all of us and smiled. "The Lord has been good to us. We have been spared," she said.

As we walked out into the road, the devastation around us was beyond belief. The hotel where Papa had begged the owner to give us accommodation had been reduced to a pile of rubble.

We would never be able to reach England now. Instead of British, there were now only German soldiers running and shouting.

4 Life Under Nazi Occupation

We were back home in Belgium. The apartment had been waiting for us. I was happy to be back in my room and my toys seemed to say, "Welcome home, Cirlake, we missed you."

Bonnemama and Bonpapa were overjoyed to see us again. No, our fears were unfounded. We had been apprehensive - perhaps life under German occupation would not be too bad after all.

Every morning, Papa went off to work. The office he had in Brussels had not been damaged by bombing. The cinemas were showing all his films and life seemed to have returned to normality.

I was now ready to go to kindergarten. It was time for me to mix with other children of my own age. "You will be doing painting, drawing and learning to read and write. That will be fun, won't it, Cirlake?" asked Mama.

I was not quite sure whether I liked the idea. "Why do I have to go to kindergarten, Mama? I want to stay with you," I said. As I looked up at her, I could see that she was not too pleased with my remark.

A few days later, there we stood in front of a large door which was opened by a smiling lady. "Do come in. The headmistress will be with you presently," she said. I looked around the room and noticed many children's paintings and drawings. The woman who came in a few minutes later apologised for keeping us waiting. "So this is Cirla. Do you like painting?" she asked.

"What a silly question!" I thought. I was determined to go home with Mama. We were shown around the school and then it was suggested I should stay for the rest of the morning. I burst into tears and clutched Mama's hand. "I want to go home!" I screamed. Mama kissed me and left.

I sat on my little stool surrounded by many other little boys and girls. As my tears dried, I started to take an interest in what was happening around me. Then it was time to go home. There was Mama. How glad I was to see her! We were going to Bonnemama for lunch.

That evening, Papa came home earlier than usual. He wanted to know whether his little girl had liked her first day at school. Mama told him about the tears. "Promise me, Cirlake, that you will not cry and upset your Mama tomorrow," he said. Yes, I would try to be brave.

As the days went by, we practically forgot about the Germans being there.

A few weeks later, some official document came through the post. It was now decreed that all Jews, young and old, would have to wear a yellow star. Mama started sewing the star onto some of my little coats. "Does everyone have to wear this star?" I asked. Mama explained that this was only meant for Jews.

Then, one day, as Mama was ready to leave me at the kindergarten, the headmistress motioned that she wanted to speak to her. She was terribly sorry to have to tell Mama that she could no longer keep me at the school. Perhaps it was for the best, because she had heard rumours that the Germans were taking Jewish children from schools. It would be safer for all concerned if I stayed at home. Well, I was quite happy about it. I preferred to be with Mama anyway.

That same evening, Papa came home and looked very sad. No, he would no longer travel to Brussels to work. I heard him say to Mama, "I cannot believe it. I am not allowed to have my own business. The swines have put a seal on my office door. I have been told that all the celluloid will be shipped to Germany to help the war effort!" I now knew who the swines were. Those horrid Germans were making all of us very unhappy.

Every morning, Papa would leave the flat. When I asked Mama, "Where is Papa going?" she answered, "He is trying to find a job, Cirlake, because otherwise we will soon have no money left to buy food and all the other things we need."

When Bonnemama came to visit us, she would always bring some fare to eat. She would show Mama how to be ingenious in the kitchen. Whatever this word meant, the result would be a carrot cake or sometimes a potato dish which would line the stomach.

One evening, when Papa came home, we knew it was good news. Yes, he had been offered a job with Philips. He was to start work next week as a salesman. Mama started to weep. I did not understand why.

A few months went by with nothing much happening. I would sit in my room and play with my dolls. Did they still love me? I had the feeling that many people avoided us. As we walked in the street, with our yellow star showing, I could see them turning their eyes away from us. Mama had said something about embarrassment - a big word for a little girl of my age to understand.

One afternoon, as we came home from Bonnemama's, Mama had a fright. Why were the lights on in the flat? Papa opened the door. His face looked grey. Why was he home so early? "Floreke, things are becoming worse. I have been given the sack. Do you know why?" His voice was harsh and he shouted, "Because I am a Jew! I saw the manager - he told me how sorry he was. It was not the company's doing." Then I heard Papa say something about a new edict the Germans had just passed. Companies were no longer allowed to employ Jews.

"What next?" I thought. "Why did the Germans do this to us?" Now that Papa was at home, Mama would say, "Jaap, take Cirlake and go for a walk." She wanted to get on with the housework. With us under her feet, it would take three times as long to do the chores.

Both Papa and I wore our star of David. He would hold his pipe with his left hand and hide the star as best he could. When it was cold, I had a little fur hand-muff and I, too, would hold it sideways, a little to the left, so that my star would not be visible either. Would I always have to wear this star and be different from other people?

One morning, Mama and Papa opened yet another letter. I looked at them both and noticed how pale their faces looked. Mama whispered, "Where will it all end?"

All Jews were to register at the Judenrat (Jewish Council). As we walked back home, I realised that some other awful incident had taken place. "What did that man put on your card?" I asked.

"It is not a card, Cirlake, it is our passport; he put a stamp on it - it says Jew." Was the star not sufficient - what else would have the word Jew on it?

Every time the postman delivered his letters to our flat, I became very quiet. From time to time, there was a letter from Amsterdam, from Oma and Opa. "When are we going to visit Oma and Opa?" I asked. Not for a long time, was the answer.

Then it happened again - a big envelope. The message was clear - it was addressed to Papa. It read:

> "You are to report to your nearest railway station on...........
> Bring with you a razor, toothbrush, toothpaste and small towel.
> The German Reich needs your services.
> Your family will not be harmed, if you follow this guidance."

Mama begged Papa not to go. She would go to see Mevrouw Workhom, the mother of an old schoolfriend of Papa's. Mama knew that her son was an influential man at the Judenrat. She would speak to the old lady and ask her to persuade her son to cross off Papa's name from the list.

That same afternoon, Papa and I stayed at home. "Be careful, Floreke," he said, as Mama left the flat.

I climbed on Papa's knee and asked him to read one of my favourite stories.

It was quite late when Mama returned. She looked so happy. "Jaap, Workhom has done it - he has crossed you off the list." My parents embraced and Mama wept as they both hugged me.

I heard them say that they would never forget how brave Workhom had been. Was it brave to cross off a name from a list? Once again I was bewildered.

As time went on, I noticed that Mama would take a small vase off the bookcase. Delft, it was. She knew someone who would be willing to buy it. Not easy, as Gentiles were not to buy anything from Jews. After the sale of the vase, we had a little more food in the house. It was Opa and Oma who had given the Delft vases. Would they be cross with Mama? I would not tell them if they asked me about it.

As usual, Bonnemama would visit us every day. She would say to Papa, "After lunch, go for a little walk with Floreke. You both need fresh air. Oy, how pale you are. Go, I will stay with my darling Cirlake."

Friends no longer visited us. I heard Mama say, "Well, some of our friends have probably gone into hiding." Then Bonnemama would ask, "Have you heard from Thylla lately?" No, Mama had not. Could you blame Gentiles for staying away? Of course not! Everyone was aware that, should they be found in the home of a Jew, they would be dealt with severely by the Germans. Sadness and loneliness seemed to envelop us.

A few weeks later, another letter was delivered by the postman. Papa opened it and I could see that his hands were trembling. As he showed the letter to Mama, I saw her bite her lower lip.

She looked at him and said, "What are you going to do, Jaap?" What could he do? The letter clearly stated that, if he refused to go to work for the German Reich, somewhere in France, the consequences for his family would be severe.

Mama cried a lot and Papa tried to comfort her.

A few days later, in the early morning, as I lay in my bed, I opened my eyes and saw Papa looking down at me. He whispered as he kissed me, "Goodbye, my dear child - look after Mama. I will be back soon."

I could not understand why Papa had to leave us. "When will Papa be back?" I asked. Mama simply said, "Soon, Cirlake, soon."

One morning, as Mama and I arrived at my grandparents' house, a neighbour came towards us. She looked agitated and spoke to Mama. "The Boches have taken away your parents; come into my house, just for a moment."

Mama's whole frame started to shake violently. She cried out, "My parents! My parents! Oh God help me!" She sobbed uncontrollably. I did not know what to do. I took her hand and kissed it - I so wanted her to stop crying.

The woman spoke gently to Mama. "You must be strong, my dear, for the sake of your child," she said.

We walked back to our flat. Mama made some strong coffee for herself and a cup of hot milk for me.

That same evening, we had a visit from my grandparents' neighbour. She came to tell us that the German special outfit, who were responsible for sealing the doors of Jewish homes, would be coming round in two days' time. Did Mama want to take any belongings out of the house? This would be the only opportunity she would get.

My favourite Aunt Yetta, who was unmarried and lived with my grandparents, came to stay with us for two nights. She had gone to work and, on her return home, was met by the kindly neighbour who told her what had happened.

Mama and her sister talked a great deal in whispers.

A few days later, when I asked Mama, "Where is Aunt Yetta?" she just replied, "She is in a safe place, Cirlake."

There we were - in front of my grandparents' house. We did not have long to wait. A car stopped and a few Germans got out. Mama took me by the hand. We approached a young German who seemed to be in charge. "Bonjour, Monsieur," Mama said. Yes, what did she want? "Could I come in with you, Monsieur? I have left some of my personal belongings in my parents' house. May I pick them up?"

As he looked at Mama, he answered in perfect French, "Of course, Madame, we are not all ogres."

Mama filled the bag she had brought with her, with as many items of silverware she could cram into it. When the young German came back from inspecting all the rooms in the house, he took her by the arm. His face was only inches away from hers when he said, "Madame, you are a lovely young woman. Take my advice - do not stay in this town with your young child."

"Why are you telling me this, Monsieur?" replied Mama.

He smiled and just said, "Well, you see, I am not German - I come from Alsace. Does that answer your question, Madame?"

We left the house, which was sealed up. I knew, somehow, that this was a place we would never return to.

That same evening, our nice neighbour, the old gentleman who lived above us, came to visit. As he walked in, I saw that he held a gold chain and a diamond ring in his hand. "Madame Italiaander," he said, "I want you to have these. I have no family in this country. I am old. If the Nazis take me, I do not think I stand much of a chance." As he left, I saw that Mama had tears in her eyes.

The first time I saw Cissie again, I remembered how we had met on our journey through France. She had also tried to reach England but had failed. Her husband, Aaron, was now in a work camp somewhere in France - perhaps the same place Papa had gone to.

She told Mama how terrified she was at having to stay in her large flat all on her own.

It was agreed that Cissie would spend daytime with us and we would take her home late afternoons. Now that Bonnemama and Bonpapa were no longer there, Mama felt that she owed it to them to help one of their friends.

Mama had Belgian nationality and, therefore, a Belgian passport. For the time being, she felt safer than most Jews. She had told Cissie why. "You see, Queen Elizabeth of the Belgians, the Queen Mother, is giving us her personal protection. She calls us her Belgian Jews." Cissie did not understand why the Germans would take any notice of this elderly lady. It was quite simple. Before becoming Queen of the Belgians, she was a Saxe-Coburg, a German Princess. Her courageous stand against the Nazi regime seemed to be effective.

I, however, although born in Belgium, had Dutch nationality and, if caught by the Germans, would not qualify for any special protection.

One day, as I was playing with my dolls, I looked up and smiled at Cissie and Mama. We had just had some hot soup and bread for lunch.

Then, the doorbell rang. For a moment, we all seemed to freeze and then Mama ran into her bedroom with me. She put me on her bed and covered me with her duvet. She whispered, "Cirlake, not a sound! Stay here. Do not move until I come to get you."

Heavy footsteps stopped at the door of our flat and a voice called out, "Open up! Gestapo!"

I could hear the door being opened. A man's loud voice said, "Passports - ah, you are Belgian!" I knew he was speaking to Mama. Then it was Cissie's turn, "And you, I see you have a British passport." He laughed loudly, as he gave back both passports. In fluent English he said, "Ah, yes, you are protected by the British Crown. You, Madam, are a very

lucky lady - the German Reich considers you to be British first
and then a Jew. Are you surprised to hear me speak fluent
English? Well, I was at Oxford University before the war.
What a splendid place!"

Then, he turned round - clicked his heels and shouted, "Heil
Hitler!" and left.

As Mama came back into the bedroom, she kissed me and I
could see she was pleased with me. I had not moved nor made
a single sound. I had been a good girl.

Mama wrote regularly to her sister, Babe, who was in
hiding in Ghent. In turn, she would receive replies quite
frequently. There was never a return address on the envelope
and Mama kept her address book hidden in a drawer in her
bedroom. She would say, "No-one must know where they are,
Cirlake."

One afternoon, I found a blue envelope which had been put
through the letter box. "Mama! A letter for you!" I shouted.
What could it be?

As she read the message, I realised, from looking at the
expression on her face, that it was bad news. It read:

> "We know the address of your relatives who are in
> hiding in Ghent. We do not wish you or them any harm
> - but you must pay us 8000 francs - or else we will have
> no alternative but to inform the German authorities of
> their whereabouts.
>
> "Send a messenger with the money in cash, tomorrow
> evening. He will be met at the end of the road, on the
> corner, opposite the flower shop, in your street."

This was again a nasty letter. I could see it from Mama's
agitation. She ran downstairs to our Belgian neighbours. What
was she to do? Jews were not allowed to go out in the
evenings. If she ignored the letter, she would not be able to
forgive herself if anything happened to her relatives.

Mr. Desmet agreed to help. He would take the envelope
with the money. Could he be trusted? Who knows; was he the
blackmailer? Who else could she turn to?

After that event, Mama went to see her childhood friends.
The Arekens family had known Mama when they were
neighbours and Thylla and the Kriksman girls had practically
grown up together. Maman Arekens, a devout Catholic, would
help her, she was sure. A message was passed to Ghent. They
were to move from their present address. We no longer
received any letters from them.

Then, what a surprise - a postcard from France, from Papa.
In it he said:

> "My darling Flore,
> "I am well. Do not worry. However, I want you to take
> the child and go away for a long holiday.
>   Your loving husband,
>   Jaap."

How had Papa managed to send this card? Where could we
go? Mama had very little money left.

Could she find a Gentile who would be willing to buy yet
another of Opa's paintings? She had already sold two. Who
would be brave enough to take this risk?

Once again Mama thought of Maman Arekens. What a true
friend she was! How I loved to hear the stories of how Mama,
her sisters and Thylla had had fun together. They would climb
over the garden wall to be with each other. Then, as they
became young ladies, they went to tea dances together, Maman
Arekens keeping a watchful eye on her charges. Even now, the
old lady reminded me of a character from the fairy stories I so
enjoyed. Her tall frame, thin face, grey eyes and majestic
demeanour were those of a queen one obeyed without question.

The Arekens family did send a buyer and Mama managed to
sell another painting and some more silverware. The walls in
the drawing room started to look quite bare. Mama said it did

not really matter, as long as we could buy food. All these things were unimportant. One day we would remember these sad times, as if in a distant dream.

One afternoon, on our return from taking Cissie back home, the doorbell rang. Who could it possibly be? There she stood, Thylla, tall, long-legged with flashing brown eyes and dark brown hair piled high into a chignon. Could she come in? "Thylla, how wonderful to see you. Nothing wrong, is there?" said Mama. No, she had come to ask advice. There was this quite charming man whom she had met and now, three months later, he had proposed to her. She liked him but did not know whether it was love. What did Mama think? I was not quite sure what the discussion was all about but it was so nice to have a visitor.

A few weeks later, the postman brought a letter and, when Mama opened it, I could see that it was good news. "Cirlake, we are invited to a wedding - Thylla's wedding."

"Oh, what fun!" I thought, and the Arekens had said that we were expected to go back to their apartment to have some tea and cakes with them. I became very excited and started to jump up and down, although normally I would not behave in such a way, as Mama would become cross and scream, "Cirlake, stop it! Think of the neighbours!"

As I looked around me, I marvelled at the splendour of this vast church. There they were, Thylla and Remy, her fiancé, who would soon be her husband. Thylla wore what had been her mother's wedding dress. Maman Arekens had pinned a white lace tablecloth - the nearest to a veil - on her daughter's dark hair.

Remy looked handsome in his Sunday-best suit. He reminded me of one of those men whom I had seen on cigarette advertising posters.

Mama and I were standing at the back of the church - the Jewess and her child - the only guests at a Catholic wedding.

After the blessing and the exchange of vows, the bride and groom looked at us and smiled. Maman Arekens said, "Floreke, we shall see you back at the flat."

It was a lovely party and the food was, I thought, like in the fairy tales; fit for a king. We laughed and chatted and for a brief moment we had the strange feeling that all the sadness and turmoil were pictures of the imagination, or better still, just a nightmare.

Then it was time for us to go home, before darkness fell.

What a happy day it had been! We had not seen any Germans either, thank God!

It had been a long day and I happily went to bed. Now that Papa was not there, I slept in the big bed with Mama.

At two o'clock in the morning, I woke up. Mama was standing near the window. She had pulled aside the curtain to look out. A little light from the streetlamps below shone into the room. I heard German voices shouting in the street, "Where are those Jews?" I got out of bed and stood near Mama. I could see several removal vans. People were made to climb into them and I heard the cries of children. I slipped my hand into Mama's and heard her whisper, "Dear God, please help us."

As the voices became louder, I realised that the German soldier with the torch in his hand was looking for more Jews. He stopped at our apartment block and shouted, "No Jews here!" A few minutes later, silence descended upon the street. They had made a mistake; they had not searched the building - we were safe for the time being!

Very early, that same morning, Mama said, "We are going to get dressed now, Cirlake." I looked at myself in the mirror and smiled. I was wearing several dresses, one on top of the other, and liked the look of my coat - no star of David, Mama had taken it off. No, we would not take any suitcases with us.

Mama's big black handbag was all she carried. As she locked the door, I held my favourite doll against me. "Goodbye flat, see you again soon," I said.

"Are we taking the tram, Mama?" I asked. No, it was too dangerous. There would be Germans everywhere. They would be on the look-out for Jews who might have escaped them.

"Where are we going? Is it still far, Mama?" I asked.

"No. Be brave, Cirlake. We shall soon be at Maman Arekens'," she answered.

When we arrived at the Arekens' flat, Mama rang the bell. A head appeared at the window and a hand motioned to let us know that she was coming down. When the door was opened, Mama simply said, "The Boches came in the early hours. They have taken everyone. We have nowhere to go." The tall woman looked at us and said, "Entrez, chère Flore. You and the child will be safe in my home."

Maman Arekens' flat was on the fourth floor. It was a spacious flat. From the windows of the drawing-room one could see the leafy avenue. The buildings on the opposite side were clearly visible. As Mama and I sat down on the settee, Maman Arekens explained that the Gestapo had moved into one of these buildings.

"Cirlake, promise me you will not go near the window - we must be very careful," she said.

Remy and Thylla, who lived on the third floor, came upstairs. They were in touch with the Resistance. A few telephone calls were made and we were told not to worry.

The plan was simple. Remy would take us to the railway station. He would walk on ahead and, should we be caught, he would phone our relatives in Ghent to warn them and they would then know what to do.

The next morning, we set off very early. At the station, Mama took our tickets. Soon, we were sitting comfortably in an empty compartment. As we were about to leave, the door was flung open. A youth dressed in a very smart uniform climbed in. I recognised the clothes - it was something to do with Hitler. Mama had mentioned that some of the young Belgians had joined a group similar to the Hitler Jugend.

I knew this boy - he was the son of the cleaning lady of one of Mama's Jewish neighbours. He smiled at us and nodded. We did not speak but when I looked up at Mama's face I could see that she had become very pale. The train stopped and the youth left our carriage. Would the Gestapo be waiting for us at the next stop?

We continued our journey without any further incidents.

As we left the station, we saw no traffic and the streets looked deserted.

"Why is Aunt Yetta not here?" I asked Mama. She just shook her head - she did not know. I started to cry. I knew that we did not have any idea of where our relatives lived. Had we been abandoned?

Then we saw her. She came running towards us. "I had to go into a shelter - we have just had a bomb alert. Thank God you are still here!" she exclaimed.

We must have walked for about twenty minutes when we stopped at a small apartment building. "Here we are," said Aunt Yetta. She opened the front door and told us to go quietly up the narrow staircase. At the top, there was another door. We rang the bell. Babe, Mama's youngest sister, smiled as she saw us. "Come in! Thank God, we are all together now!" she said.

5 In Hiding

Uncle Jacques, Babe's husband, stood up. He wore no shoes. He looked thin and tired. He spoke in a whisper, "Yes, dear Flore, here I am."

I looked at his right hand. It was horrible - red and swollen. I saw a thumb and three fingers. Mama spoke very quietly, "Jacques, you have escaped - what about Jaap?"

What could he say? They had been together in the work camp until his escape.

As he spoke, he no longer seemed to be in the same room with us. He was back in France working on the railway track. Fancy he and Jaap, professional men, expected to do heavy manual work! The German soldiers, with their machine guns at the ready, watched the prisoners who laboured hours on end, with little food. Boiled potato peelings and anything that moved, was their diet.

Then, one day, overcome with exhaustion, he did not see the train coming towards them. His reactions were slow - he looked up but too late. His hand was caught between two buffers. He screamed and fainted. As he opened his eyes, he could see Jaap kneeling beside him. A German guard lifted him up and, half an hour later, he was lying in the basement of the nearby hospital. There was not much light and he could barely see his surroundings. What he did notice was that he was completely naked. There were no bedclothes on the bed. Although he missed a finger, he felt a throbbing pain. Some male nurse approached and told him that a surgeon would sew up the wound. Yet another hell to endure!

Back at the work camp, Jaap asked to see the Commandant. As he was shown into the room, he did not look at the German until spoken to.

The Commandant was a stocky man. He had a round face and piercing eyes. As he looked up at the prisoner, he spoke quickly, "What do you want?"

"I would like to know what has happened to my brother-in-law who had an accident on the rail track, yesterday afternoon," said Jaap.

"Ah, yes, the prisoner was taken to the hospital down the road. We take good care of our workers," answered the Commandant with a sardonic smile.

"I would like to ask your permission to visit my brother-in-law, Herr Kommandant," said Jaap.

The German looked astounded at such a request. However, he felt in a generous mood, just then.

"Well, I agree to let you go on one condition. I will not even send a guard with you - but remember, if you do not return after your visit, each day that you are absent, one of the prisoners will be shot."

Jaap gave his word. He would not try to escape.

In the hospital, the Jews were separated from the other patients - Gentiles on the ground floor and Jews in the basement.

Jacques was lying on his bed and, in the dim light, Jaap could see that one of his fingers had been amputated.

He whispered, "Jaap, it is good to see you," and then he added, "I am going to escape from this hell - you too must leave this place."

Jaap came to visit him several times. He remained silent when Jacques mentioned about wanting to escape.

One night he ran to a nearby farm. God alone knows what the people thought when they saw this weird apparition. Jacques knew that these particular farmers would do their best to help. He had seen the woman on numerous occasions near the perimeter of the fence. When the guard's back was turned, she had made a sign as if to say, "We are friends."

Clothes were provided for him. A train ticket was bought and he had been given an address to contact in Belgium. Here he was - back with his wife and child.

I looked at my cousin, Danielle, and envied her. How lucky she was - her Papa had come home!

The apartment was small but clean. Four adults and two children slept, ate and washed in accommodation which was suitable for only three people.

The landlady from whom the flat was rented was told that Aunt Babe, her husband, my cousin Danielle and Aunt Yetta were terrified by the bombardments in Antwerp. Ghent was a safer place. She quite agreed.

The days passed quite slowly.

Every morning, Uncle Jacques would get dressed. After putting on his shoes, he would thump down the stairs, to make it appear as if he was going to work. Then, he would take off his shoes and creep up the stairs, making sure that he had not been noticed - the man of the house going off in the morning. In the evening, he would descend the stairs silently and go up again noisily.

"You, Cirlake, must be a good girl and not make any noise," I was told.

Danielle, my cousin, and I would dress and undress two dolls which we shared.

When we tired of this game, we would watch Uncle Jacques play patience. I knew that it was pointless to ask Mama whether we could go out.

One morning, as we had just finished breakfast, there was a loud knock on the door. We all sat motionless. A man's voice called out, "Police! Is there anyone at home?" This was repeated several times and then we heard someone go down the stairs and the footsteps became fainter.

What was to be done? Aunt Babe said, "I shall go down to the landlady and tell her that I have been lying down with a terrible migraine."

When she returned, she looked troubled, "Well, this is it! We have to leave as soon as possible. Apparently, a murder has taken place in this road - an important lawyer. The police are making door to door inquiries."

The rent had been paid and all of us would just disappear.

Mama gathered together our few belongings. In the meantime, Aunt Yetta had contacted the Resistance. We were all to go our separate ways. We said our goodbyes and left the flat.

It was early afternoon as Mama and I walked towards the park. It was here that we had to wait for someone to come to take us to a safe place.

We waited and waited and went from one bench to another, avoiding the German guards who were patrolling the park.

We had had no lunch and my stomach felt empty. Mama looked at me and said, "Do you know, Cirlake, I believe it is Yom Kippur today." She looked very solemn and explained that, on this day, we asked God for forgiveness - for all the bad things we had done during the year. I did not feel that I had been all that naughty!

A tall man came towards us and said, "Liberté, I am a friend. Please follow me at a distance."

We seemed to have walked for quite a long while, when at last we stopped in front of a large house.

A grey-haired woman, looking harassed and wearing a multi-coloured apron, opened the door. "Ah, there you are. Come in," she said. Did we know what the establishment was? "This is a boarding house for businessmen and students. I have several lodgers. I take it, Madame, that you understand what is expected from you?" Mama just nodded. Yes, she would help in the kitchen and her duties would include those of the chambermaid who had just left. She would not receive any wages but just board and lodging. Then the woman turned to me and said, "You look like a well-behaved little girl."

We were shown to a small room which looked clean but rather bare. The bed was big enough to take an adult and a small child. There was no running water - just a big washbowl with a jug full of water. Mama washed my hands and face and combed my hair and we went down to have our first meal of the day.

Every morning, we got up before the other residents. Mama would help to prepare breakfast and, after the washing up was done, she would start making the beds and clean out all the rooms. I would follow her around and pretend to be invisible as, otherwise, Mama could not finish her chores in time to help to prepare lunch.

I liked going into one room in particular. It was Monsieur de Lacroix's room. He was a student at the university and his room was full of books and pretty rugs on the floor. As he left in the morning, he would always smile and greet us with a kind word.

"When you do my room, Madame, do feel free to have a rest and, should you want to borrow one of my books or magazines, please do so," he said. On several occasions, he had muttered, "When will we be rid of the Boches?" Mama's face had remained impassive. Was he guessing? Could he be trusted?

The kind Catholic priest, who visited the boarding house regularly, would greet Mama with the words, "How are you today, my child?" Why did he call Mama 'my child', I wondered.

Several weeks went by. One evening, the owner of the boarding house said that she wanted a word with Mama. "My dear, I am afraid that I can no longer keep you here," she said. One of the lodgers was becoming suspicious and was asking too many questions. "I shall make a few 'phone calls and we shall

Flore and Jaap on their wedding day (1935)

(back row, left to right) Henri, Madeleine and Oncle Jean;
(front row, left to right) Suzy (Cirla), Flore, Tante Betty and
Gilberte Liem (1944)

(back row, left to right) A friend of the family, Tante Betty, Gilberte, Tom Young, a British soldier, M Sendyk (a friend);
(front row, left to right) Flore, Oncle Jean, Henri's wife, Suzy wearing the British soldier's beret, Mme Sendyk (a friend) and Madeleine - the Liberation (1944)

(left to right) Flore, Madeleine (in the foreground), Tom and one of the British soldiers who liberated Ghent. A bottle of champagne was dug up from the garden! (1944)

Suzy at school after the war (c. 1945)

Tante Betty and Suzy in the garden - back in Ghent to celebrate
Tante Betty's eightieth birthday (December 1969)

(left to right) Rosemary Young (Tom's daughter), Gilberte, Jean-Marie (Tante Betty's grandson), Tom, Tante Betty, Joseph (Gilberte's husband), Madeleine and Vivianne (Tante Betty's second grandchild), Boulevard du Chateau No. 5 (December 1969)

Thylla and Remy in their home (1983)

Painting of Amsterdam by Mauritz Italiaander (1926) bought at an auction after the Second World War

try to find you another place to go to." Mama looked weary and said, "Thank you Madame. You are very kind."

A middle-aged buxom lady, dressed in a tight-fitting black coat, wearing thick spectacles, looked down at me. "What is your name, child?" she enquired. "Cirlake, Madame," I replied.

"Oh, that will never do! We shall call you 'Suzy'." From then on, I was known as Suzy - a good French-sounding Christian name!

"My name is Betty Liem. You and your Mama may call me 'Tante Betty'," said the woman.

She spoke quickly and decisively. "Floreke! You and Suzy will follow me. Please do not speak to me whilst we are on the road. I shall pay your fares when we are on the tram."

I waved goodbye as we left the boarding house.

We followed Tante Betty at a distance and when we got onto the tram Mama chose a seat near the exit. We did not speak. I sat on her knee and rested my head against her shoulder.

As we got off the tram, we could see the woman in the distance. She seemed to be walking towards a building in front of which a German soldier was pacing up and down. Was this a trap? No. We breathed a sigh of relief. She turned the corner and crossed the bridge. Then we saw the big house. She went in using her front door key.

We were to follow a few minutes later. There it was, number five, Boulevard du Château. We rang the bell and the door was opened. Safe once again!

As I looked around me, I was standing in a large dining room. On the walls, I could see many paintings. A white lace tablecloth covered the table and there were about eight sturdy chairs standing like soldiers round it. The room overlooked a small garden. It was pleasant, light and spacious.

An elderly gentleman stood up as Mama and I came in. "This is my husband. You may call him 'Oncle Jean'," said Tante Betty. He seemed older than his wife but his demeanour was that of a forty-year old man. He was not very tall but I liked his face which smiled at me. His brown eyes were kind and gentle as he looked at both of us. "Welcome to our home - you will be safe here," said Oncle Jean.

Then Tante Betty turned to us and said, "These are our two daughters; this is Madeleine, the elder, and this is Gilberte, our teenager, who is still at school."

Madeleine was tall and blond. Her determined features somehow revealed strength of character. As I looked up at her, I could see her pale eyes smiling at me. Gilberte had flame-coloured hair and blue eyes. She was much shorter than her sister. She came towards me and took my hand. "Do you want to go upstairs to meet our cat?" she asked.

"Oh yes, please!" I exclaimed.

The house was very big. The front room had been converted into a shop. Tante Betty was a furrier and had quite a number of private clients who came regularly to have their fur coats repaired and sometimes remodelled.

In the upstairs drawing room, there were a number of armchairs and, in one corner, stood a most beautiful grand piano. "This is mine," said Gilberte. She sat down and quickly played a piece of music, which was very lovely, I thought. When she had finished, she looked at me and said, "Do you know what this is called? It is the Polonaise by Chopin." Whoever this 'Chopin' person was, I liked the tune very much - better than the Frère Jacques tune I could play!

As I turned round, there he was, the most adorable cat I had ever seen. "This is Fripon (meaning 'Rascal'). Say hello to Suzy," said Gilberte. The cat just licked my hand and purred.

Then it was time to go upstairs to what would be our bedroom for many months. The room overlooked the back garden. It was a spacious room with a large bed. In one corner stood a tall wardrobe and in the other, a table with a basin and water jug. As I looked up, I saw the cross hanging just above the bed. I asked Mama, "Why is this man nailed to the cross?" She replied simply, "This is Jesus; this is a Catholic house, chérie." Later on, I was told that Jesus was the son of God and that Catholic people prayed to him. I felt very sorry for him on that cross!

Mama did not call me Suzy. I suppose she felt happier just using the term, 'chérie' - after all, it meant 'darling'.

After having freshened up, we went down to the dining room to have supper.

Apart from the Liem family, there were other guests. As we were introduced to them, Tante Betty explained, "This is Henri. He has been with us for a number of months. He escaped over the rooftops one night when the Gestapo came to arrest him. He has been very active in the Resistance movement." He looked like a nice man to me. He was tall with a big chest and a small head. He nodded and smiled at me and Mama. He spoke to Mama, "I am so glad you will be joining us here - may I call you Flore?"

"This is Gust," said Tante Betty. He was the other guest in the house. I did not think he was very handsome. He had a pale face and a pointed nose and very thin lips.

"Gust is here because he declined the invitation to go to work for the Nazis," said Tante Betty. He just grinned and seemed to be in a hurry to start eating his supper.

The food was absolutely delicious. I enjoyed the meat stew with the mashed potatoes and the pancakes were yummy. Mama could not believe her eyes. Everyone commented on what a good eater I was. I remembered the times Mama had been cross when I only wanted to eat what Bonnemama prepared.

Before going to bed, I kissed my new family goodnight. Tante Betty made a sign of the cross on my forehead and whispered, "Goodnight, Suzy - God be with you."

As Mama tucked me up in bed, I closed my eyes and was at peace with the world.

Our day would start quite early. Every morning, Tante Betty would go to church and, on her return, we would all have breakfast together.

Then Mama would help with the dishes and afterwards she would do some sewing for Tante Betty. She was soon able to repair fur coats and this made her feel she was contributing in a positive way.

Madeleine and Mama would also clean the house and I would be told, "Go and play with Fripon, Suzy." How I loved my new companion!

Gilberte would go to school every day and I would wait for her to come home in the afternoon. She too was my friend but at times she could be very bossy and get me into trouble.

I remembered the time she had told me to go into the pantry and cut off some pieces from the Sunday joint, so that we could play with Fripon and feed him with real food. She had told me to put the meat into Tante Betty's wardrobe so that it was kept in a safe place. A few days later, Tante Betty had opened her wardrobe and the disgusting smell of the meal meant for Fripon had led her to discover our special hiding place.

Mama had wanted to hit me but Oncle Jean had said he would explain to me that I must not do such a naughty thing again.

I heard him say, "Floreke, we do not want our neighbours to be alerted to the fact that we have a young child in the house."

Gust and Henri would sit for hours trying to build a special radio which could receive BBC news bulletins from London. I would watch them and wondered whether they were clever enough to build such a complicated piece of equipment. One day, they announced that they had been successful. From that day onwards, they would give us the latest news.

Oncle Jean would go into his bedroom and sit at a big table where he would make complicated drawings of strategic places to be bombed by the RAF. I was not quite sure what that meant.

Weeks went by. The one thing I found very hard was to remember not to go near the window. Mama would repeat again and again, "Chérie, promise me not to go near the window." I knew why. If anyone saw me, they might go and tell the nasty soldiers and then we would all be taken away and something really bad would happen to us!

One day Henri told Mama, "You know, Flore, I am a very patient man. I will be happy to teach Suzy to read and write." Everyone agreed; the child needed to be educated. If they meant by that, reading and writing, I could do without it!

Lessons started and Henri put on his teacher's face. I could not understand what I was supposed to learn! Numbers, to make sums, letters which became words if you put them together; it all seemed far too complicated for me. I wanted to be left alone. Soon I discovered that all this learning would come to an end if I cried loudly. What was all the commotion about? Henri was told by Oncle Jean to stop the lessons immediately. I went back to playing with Fripon.

One evening, at dinner time, I listened carefully to the conversation the adults were having. What if the Nazis raided the house? Well, Floreke, Henri and Gust could jump over the garden wall. The child would have to stay behind and the Nazis would be told that the little girl was the daughter of a cousin who had died in childbirth. I knew that they were talking about me. Then Oncle Jean turned to me and said, "Suzy, your Mama will not be able to take you with her, if she has to escape. You will have to pretend not to be able to hear nor speak, if the Nazis should ask you questions." So, that was what they meant when they mentioned about being deaf and dumb.

From time to time, the heavy bombardments forced all of us into the cellar, where we were often told to stay the rest of the night.

When Mama had done all the chores and sewing, she would sometimes sit down at the grand piano and play a piece of music which reminded her of her youth. The Polonaise was my favourite. I thought of it as my song of freedom.

6 Tom

A few more weeks passed by. As Tante Betty sat down at the dinner table, she seemed strangely preoccupied. She looked at all of us and said, "I want you to listen very carefully to what I have to say. This may come as a surprise and you must tell me frankly how you feel."

She had been approached by the Resistance. A young British airman needed a safe place to stay until the end of the war.

"Jean and I want to help this young man but, if you people feel that you cannot cope with the extra danger, then you are free to leave and we shall try to find you another place to shelter." Gust was the only one who said he preferred to go elsewhere. Mama and Henri felt it was only right that we should agree to Tom joining our little group.

I was thrilled. What would this pilot person be like? Would he be wearing a special uniform? I was looking forward to having a new friend to talk to.

A few days later, Tante Betty went off to church, as usual.

After the service, she decided to go to the address given to her by the Resistance. She had memorised the number of the house and the name of the road. As she rang the doorbell, a young woman opened the door. She was shown into a small but comfortable flat which was furnished with what she recognised as beautiful antiques.

"Bonjour, Madame," said an elderly lady in a wheelchair. She smiled at Tante Betty and continued, "This is our young British airman, Tom. I take it that you do not speak English fluently, so I shall explain to him what you expect him to do."

Tom was to follow Tante Betty. They would take a tram. She would pay his fare but he was to speak to no-one and certainly not to her.

All of us were waiting for the new arrival. Henri hoped the new resident would be more congenial than Gust, with whom he had quarrelled quite a lot lately.

There he stood, a medium-height, slimly-built young man. Under a working man's cloth cap, I could see ginger hair, a freckled face and blue eyes which looked at all of us in wonderment. Why the welcoming party?

Henri, in his usual outgoing manner, went towards the young man and shook his hand.

Mama said, "I am Flore and this is my little girl, Suzy. Do sit down. Would you like a cup of tea?" As he smiled, I could see strong white teeth but why was he not wearing a smart pilot's uniform?

"Are you very tired?" asked Mama. Yes, he felt exhausted. He would very much like to have a rest. He laughed when Tante Betty said, "Tom was shotten down by the Nazis and his plane fell from the sky in the village of Bavegem." He would tell us all about his adventures later on that evening.

As we all sat round the dinner table, Tom looked relaxed as he began to tell his story. As the other people in the room did not understand English that well, especially when spoken with a Scottish accent, Mama acted as interpreter.

"As you probably know from Tante Betty, the Resistance got in touch with her. Well, here I am. My name is Tom Young. I come from Dunblane. I am Scottish and 19 years old.

"As we were returning from our bombing raid on Russelheim in the Rhur, our Lancaster bomber was flying back to good old England. I was sitting next to John Lawrie, our pilot. I was, in fact, co-pilot. We were exhausted and eager to get back to base. Then, I saw the German JU88 night fighter. John tried to take evasive action but we were hit. I could feel the plane shudder and I knew that we would have to abandon the aircraft. John looked at me and told me that we were operating on only one engine.

"'Everybody bale out!' was the order. He reached for his watch and his words were, 'Tom, if I don't make it, give this to my Ma, back in New Zealand.'

"I guess windows and roofs must have been damaged when our bomber crashed. I remembered what I had been taught by the RAF. Run as far as possible from where your aircraft has crashed. It must have been about 1.30 a.m. I kept on running, with my parachute under my arm. I must admit, I felt very scared. Finally, I buried my parachute and lay down in a ditch to sleep. It was dawn when I woke up. I decided to walk hoping, somehow, to get to the sea. As I walked through the countryside, I realised it must be Sunday morning. I came to a village. By that time, people were coming out of church. I could see them looking at me in a funny sort of way. I suppose they had not seen an RAF uniform in this part of the world. I thought I might try out my few words of German on several of the villagers. They looked at me in disbelief and shook their heads. My poor French did not help either.

"I had the uneasy feeling that I should not push my luck; so far I had not seen any Germans.

"As I came to the edge of the village, I walked towards open fields. I looked round and could see a young man on a bike. He spoke a little English and explained that I should hide and that he wanted to help me. Did I realise that I was in danger? I waited a few hours and then I saw them coming towards me. Three young men and a very pretty girl. They had a dictionary with them, also some food and some old clothes, so that I would look less conspicuous.

"I was shown a map on which they had marked the village, Bavegem. I was to proceed to Ghent. Someone would meet me at this particular bridge. My link man would be waiting for me. The password was 'Churchill'. What else was I to do? They wished me good luck and the girl kissed me goodbye. I wonder whether I shall ever see them again."

As Tom finished his story, Tante Betty said, "Jean, open a bottle of wine and let us drink to the end of the war." Even I was allowed a sip of red wine.

Madeleine seemed much livelier since Tom joined our little group. She was in love with Tom, thought Mama. I did not quite understand what 'in love' was, but it was a nice thing, because Madeleine kept on giving me biscuits and saying could I go and play somewhere else? Maybe a few other people could be in love!

7 The Liberation

It was now summer, August 1944. We were still not allowed to go out during the day but, in the evenings, we could go into the garden for a breath of fresh air. "Suzy, if you can be very quiet, you may sit on the bench near the wall." I promised to be as quiet as a mouse.

Tom and Henri listened to the BBC news and even I was given the earphones and heard the pretty tune - Beethoven's 5th - to me it sounded like, pah, pah, pah, pah...

The news was good. Things were looking up. A few more weeks to go...

One morning as we got up, we heard the rumble of heavy trucks. Oncle Jean described what he saw from the window, "The Boches are on their way. You should see them - they no longer have that arrogant look about them. They are retreating." Soon, it would be time to take the Belgian flag and the Union Jack from under our mattresses.

Henri and Tom had heard it on the radio - the Allies had landed. Only hours to go!

What excitement. Tante Betty and Oncle Jean came into the living room. It was official; they had been told by the Resistance. The Canadians of the Eighth Army were on the outskirts of Ghent. The flags were hoisted. We all ran out into the street. Strangers came up to us and people wanted to know who we were.

How wonderful! Where was the British pilot? They wanted to shake hands with Tom. Was this the Jewess and her young child? Which one was Henri, the Resistance worker?

Tante Betty and Oncle Jean were being hugged and congratulated.

As the tanks rolled in, young girls climbed onto them. Bottles of champagne were dug up from gardens and people were crying and singing at the same time.

This was the day we had been waiting for. We were free - free as the wind in the trees - free as the birds in the sky.

Mendel Selmanoff Kriksman - died in Auschwitz.

Soura Kriksman - died in Auschwitz.

Mauritz Italiaander - died in Auschwitz.

Rachel Italiaander - died in Auschwitz.

Jacob Italiaander - died in Auschwitz.

Epilogue

So many times I have sat at my desk and my thoughts have gone back to those dreadful years, when the wicked seemed to rule the world.

When talking with friends, Jews and Gentiles, I have answered questions - where were you during the war? What was it like to live under German occupation? What could I say? Could they really understand my feelings of sorrow?

How does one explain to people sitting round the dinner table how one's heart nearly stopped when a German voice shouted in the street. How one hid one's yellow star and hoped one would not be discovered. How one closed one's eyes before going to sleep and feared that one would be dragged out of bed in the middle of the night.

Then, after the war, there were the nightmares - seeing faces of loved ones in a crowd, practically touching them and then waking up and knowing that they were gone forever.

I am fortunate to be alive today. I am grateful to have a loving husband and to be the mother of a handsome son. When I look at my son's face, I see in it features bearing a striking resemblance to the faded photograph of my dear father, a grandfather my son never knew.

The Nazis decided that those Jews who had wedded Gentiles would not be put to death.

Eli had been taken to the transit camp in Malines (Belgium), from where he was to be sent to one of the concentration camps.

Nie, his wife, managed to trace the church where her mother had been baptised. She took the certificate to the Commandant of the camp and demanded the release of her husband.

Thus, brave Nie, saved the life of her husband, Eli.

76

Vanhemde, my father's partner, did get to England with his family. I believe he died after a long illness, twenty years ago.

Our neighbour, the old gentleman who lived in the flat above us, did not survive. I sometimes wear the chain and ring he gave to my mother. I have not forgotten him.

My aunt Yetta survived. She married a British captain, whom she met when working for ENSA (Entertainments National Services Association), at the end of the war. She died in 1990.

Oncle Jacques died in September 1968 of cancer.

Aunt Babe passed away in September 1979.

Aunt Lien and Uncle Edu were hidden by Dutch peasants and survived the war. They died some years ago.

Their daughter, Yvonne, was taken in by Dutch farmers who cared for her until the end of the war. She married an American and lives outside Paris. She has three sons.

Robert, Lien's young son by her first marriage, was taken from Amsterdam by the Nazis and died in Auschwitz.

My cousin, Danielle, married a Swiss with whom she has one daughter. They live in Geneva.

Maman Arekens died a number of years ago. Her daughter, Thylla, is now a frail old lady. She still lives in Antwerp, Belgium. Her husband, Remy, died in November 1992.

Cissie, who was in a camp for British prisoners of war, survived and lived out her last years in a home for the elderly,

in North London. Her husband, Aaron, died in one of the
concentration camps. When I visited her with my husband, she
recognised me and did not talk about the present but the past.
As I held her hand, I realised that most of the people around
her were feeble-minded and the staff too busy to listen to an old
lady recounting events which happened fifty years ago. She
died in 1991.

Gust and Henri died some years ago.

Oncle Jean died on 7th December 1962.

In December 1969, I went back to Ghent to celebrate Tante
Betty's eightieth birthday. Tom Young and his daughter were
also there. Betty Liem passed away on 23rd April 1974.

Gilberte, the younger daughter, married and has a daughter
and a married son.

Madeleine, her sister, lives in a home for the elderly. She is
in good health and helps the nuns to look after the other
residents.

Tom Young, the British airman, came with his wife, Bridie,
to my son's Barmitzvah twelve years ago. He died on 17th
August 1992.

My mother died on 10th January 1985. I remember taking
her in my arms and holding her near whilst tears streamed
down my face. "Bonnemama, I am here, Cirlake is here."
Somehow, I knew that she had waited for me, so that I could
kiss her and be with her until the end.

I have told my story to people I will never meet or know.
I have bared my soul and wept for all those who were
tormented and perished in the Holocaust.

This is a testimony to those people who gave us shelter and comfort when we needed it most.

I still remember. Who will do so after I am gone?

Appendix

On 10th May 1940, at dawn, the Germans advanced into Belgium and Holland.

German troops, about one hundred, landed silently in gliders and seized the Belgian bridges across the Albert Canal. The parachutists had trained arduously to be ready for the capture of the Belgian fortress of Eben-Emael.

At 7 a.m., an appeal for help was received by London from the Dutch and Belgian governments.

The British government authorised the destruction of the Dutch and Belgian port installations at the mouth of the Scheldt, that morning.

Shortly before midday on 11th May 1940, the Belgian defenders of Fort Eben-Emael surrendered. The superior German firepower had overwhelmed them. They had fought bravely but had lost the battle.

On 13th May 1940, General Rommel's troops advanced through Belgium and crossed the river Meuse at Dinant.

On the same day, more German troops pushed through the Ardennes and crossed the same river Meuse, further south, near Sedan, France.

It is said that the Dutch Queen Wilhelmina telephoned King George VI, at Buckingham Palace, on the same morning. When the King answered the telephone, he could hardly believe his ears. She told him that it was possible that she might be kidnapped by the Germans and that, if so, she might be used as a hostage. She wanted to join her armed forces in Zeeland. However, heavy German bombardments made this impossible. The British destroyer, 'Hereward', took her to Harwich. When she arrived in Harwich, it was explained to the Queen that nothing could be done for Holland and her people, at this stage.

The Dutch monarch was naturally very upset. She had not wanted to leave Holland.

King George VI went to meet Queen Wilhelmina at Liverpool Street Station in London. He saw before him a determined Dutch woman, who would stand up to German tyranny.

On 15th May, at the Dutch port of Ijmuiden, British troops were still landing, in the hope of being able to help the Dutch resistance.

A bus carrying two hundred Jewish children from Amsterdam reached the port.

Mevrouw Wijsmuller, a Dutch woman, had brought them to the port. Many of the children were, in fact, German Jews who had been taken to Holland before the war.

The children were taken on board a ship. At 9 o'clock that evening, the ship's radio operator heard the sad news - the Dutch had capitulated.

The children were given refuge in Britain.

On 27th May 1940, Operation Dynamo had started. The Dunkirk beaches were crowded by British troops waiting for boats to take them back to England.

The German air attacks were so fierce that the troops wondered what the RAF were doing to protect them.

Hundreds of craft came from ports and seaside resorts of southern Britain. Many small craft were bombed as they reached the open sea. 299 British warships and 420 other vessels evacuated 335,490 officers and men.

General Alexander, with the Senior Naval Officer at Dunkirk, Captain Tennant, toured the harbour and shore line in a fast motor boat. They wanted to make sure that not a single soldier was left behind. Then they returned to the quayside and embarked for Great Britain.

At 11 p.m., that same night, the Belgian front was broken. The uninterrupted German aerial and artillery bombardment had been effective.

King Leopold of the Belgians asked for an armistice. The envoy who had been sent, returned five hours later - Germany demanded unconditional surrender. The King consulted his Army Staff and accepted. Belgium had resisted for eighteen days.

Many Belgians were dismayed. However, what could be done? The Belgian army had ceased to exist.

Some Belgian fishing vessels did not surrender but joined the armada of little ships.

On 31st May, the Lydie Suzanne took on board 105 men and brought them back to Dover. The Zwaluw (Swallow) had 58 men, the Cor Jesu 274 men, the Jonge Jan 270 men and the A5 234 men. Thus, some courageous Belgian fishermen fought back, as well as they could, against an invader who would prove to be harsh and ruthless during the occupation of their small country.

Back in England, Churchill spoke in the House of Commons and said that no attempt should be made to pass judgement on the Belgian King's action. However, it should be said that many Belgians felt betrayed.

Churchill, in his determination to persuade France to carry on the fight, warned the French that it should be realised that, if Germany defeated either Ally, the conquered would be treated as slaves.

On 3rd June 1940, the German Air Force bombed Paris. 254 people were killed, 195 civilians and 59 soldiers. Many of the civilians were schoolchildren. A truck in which they had taken refuge had received a direct hit.

At about 6.30 a.m., on 14th June 1940, German military vehicles arrived at the Place de la Concorde. A German headquarters was set up at the Hotel Crillon, a top hotel in this splendid city.

700,000 Parisians were awakened by German loudspeakers informing them that a curfew would be enforced starting at 8 p.m. that same evening. Earlier, two million Parisians had fled the city.

That same morning, Parisians saw, to their dismay, not their beloved tricolore but a large Swastika flag hanging from beneath the Arc de Triomphe.

A German military band, in resplendent uniforms, marched down the Champs Elysées and it was clear for everyone to see that this was meant to be a victory march.

At noon, on 17th June 1940, Marshall Pétain (who had fought at Verdun during the First World War), formed a new government, after the resignation of Paul Reynaud, Prime Minister of France.

Pétain broadcast to the French people, to inform them that negotiations with the Germans for an armistice were in progress.

On 17th June 1940, yet another evacuation of British troops from France took place. This time it was called Operation Ariel. In the eight days between 16th and 24th June, 163,225 people had embarked and were on their way to England.

At 6 p.m., on 18th June 1940, General De Gaulle broadcast from London to the French people. He assured all those listening that, although France was under German occupation, France would one day be victorious.

Those Frenchmen - officers, engineers and skilled workmen who were in Britain - were to get in touch with him. Frenchmen in France and elsewhere would resist!

Brigadier-General De Gaulle was in exile. He was forty-nine years old. He spoke with fervour and all those who heard him took heart and felt inspired.

On 20th June 1940, a French delegation travelled to Rethondes, in the forest of Compiègne, in order to negotiate the Armistice with the Germans.

The French negotiators had no idea where the negotiations were to be held. At 3.30 p.m., on 21st June, they found themselves in the same railway coach in which the Germans had signed the surrender at the end of the First World War.

Hitler was jubilant. He sat silently, as General Keitel read out to the French the Armistice terms. There was no question of discussion, only complete submission to the terms. Ten minutes later, Hitler left the railway coach. The Armistice was, in fact, signed on the 22nd June.

Hitler was now the conqueror of Poland, Norway, Denmark, Holland, Belgium and France.

He was now more than ever determined to bring Britain to her knees.

At 3.30 a.m., on 23rd June 1940, Hitler left his headquarters at Bruly-de-Pesche (Belgium), and flew to Paris.

This would be the one and only visit he would make to the French capital.

During his tour of Paris, he ordered the destruction of two First World War monuments - the statue of General Mangin, a war hero of 1918, and the British nurse Edith Cavell's memorial. She had remained in Brussels after German occupation in 1915. During her stay in the Belgian capital, she had helped to smuggle Allied troops to the Dutch border. She was caught by the Germans and was executed by firing squad.

Hitler's order was carried out immediately.

After having seen Paris, Hitler asked Albert Speer, his architect, to resume work on new public buildings and monuments in Berlin. Paris need not be destroyed; Berlin would be made far more beautiful!

In June 1942, Adolf Eichmann informed his aides of his plan to deport 40,000 Jews from France, the same number from Holland and 10,000 from Belgium. They would be sent to a place called Oswiecim. Ninety per cent of the victims in this camp were Jews.

After the war, we know this hell by the name of Auschwitz.

It is said that the Judenrat (Jewish Council) - some of whose members were appointed by the Gestapo itself from among well-known, respected and wealthy Jews of the community - made it easier for the Nazis to keep the Jews under control. The lists of names certainly helped the Nazis to trace people without much effort.

Perhaps it was thought that co-operation would make the regime less harsh, which soon proved to be a fallacy.

However, some leaders of the Judenrat tried their best to use their official position to help others in the Jewish community. They put their lives at risk in trying to save fellow Jews and some also ended up in the extermination camps.

By January 1943, a police force of 25,000 men was operating in France. The Milice, as it was called, worked together with the Gestapo and had, as its task, to arrest suspected members of the French Resistance and also to round up Jews.

When Dr. Mengele reached Auschwitz on 25th May 1943, more Dutch Jews arrived from Holland - in fact, a further 2,862. At the end of May, a total of 8,000 Dutch Jews had been deported to the camp. Two thousand Croatian Jews, ten thousand Greek Jews and 395 Jews from Berlin were also brought to the camp.

It should be noted that, when a typhoid epidemic broke out in the Gypsies' barracks, all the 1,042 were driven to the gas chambers where they perished.

In the summer of 1943, the Germans began the destruction of the evidence of mass murder, as some of Hitler's subordinates were no longer confident that the Führer could retain the domination of Europe. However, whilst this was going on, the murders were stepped up, whilst Jewish slave labourers were taken to the pits, where they were ordered to take gold rings and extract gold teeth from the corpses and then forced to burn the remains.

In January 1944, American and British aircraft were dropping arms to Resistance groups in Belgium, Holland, France and Italy.

On 6th June 1944, just before dawn, the Allies came ashore in Normandy.
The Americans landed at 'Utah' beach using amphibious tanks.
The British landed at 'Gold' and 'Sword' beaches.
The Canadian troops came ashore at 'Juno' beach.
At 'Omaha' beach, the 35,000 American men were pinned down by the German defenders and had a far more difficult time than the other Allied forces.
155,000 Allied troops had come ashore by midnight. This was D-Day.
On 20th June 1944, roundabout midnight, half a million Allied soldiers had gone ashore in Normandy. Four thousand had been killed in the first two weeks of fighting.
London was informed that the French Resistance were planning an 'uprising' and that more arms and ammunition were needed. Churchill ordered that the Resistance should be given what they required.

At the beginning of June 1944, Jews were still being deported to Auschwitz from France, Italy, Holland and Hungary.
Four Jews managed to escape from Auschwitz and the news of the mass killings reached neutral Switzerland.
As a result of the escape, a request was made to London and Washington for the railway lines leading to Auschwitz to be bombed. Names of the stations on those lines were included in the appeal.

Churchill was sympathetic to the appeal. However, it was feared by the British Air Ministry that many British airmen's lives would be lost should this bombing be attempted. In any case, the bombing would have to be done during daylight, by the Americans.

In Washington, four separate appeals to bomb the lines were rejected.

Nothing was done and the transportations continued.

On 27th August 1944, Léon Degrelle, the Flemish Fascist leader, was bestowed with the Oak Leaves to the Knight's Cross, indeed a great honour for a foreign volunteer, and presented by the Führer himself.

Raoul Wallenberg, a Swedish diplomat, organised Swedish visas for 630 Hungarian Jews.

Up till this present day, it is not known what happened to him after the Russians liberated that part of Europe. It is said that he was taken prisoner by the Russians and that he died somewhere in Russia.

His heroism has been acknowledged by the State of Israel.

The Allies entered Brussels on 3rd September 1944.
Antwerp was liberated on 4th September 1944.

On 5th September 1944, the excited voice of the announcer on Brussels radio informed listeners that Germany had surrendered.

The Belgian Independent Parachute Company of the Special Air Service were dropped behind German lines, to help the Belgian Resistance.

Towns and villages were liberated but the Nazis continued with the execution of their captives until the end.

American troops took control of the Fort of Eben-Emael on 10th September 1944. The Germans surrendered quite quickly.

Despite the breakdown of Hitler's forces in France and Belgium, the Führer informed his generals that there would be an offensive against the Allies and that this would take place through the Ardennes, the port of Antwerp (Belgium) being its objective.

Although this appendix deals mainly with events related to Belgium, Holland and France, the writer would like to mention an incident which took place as late as September 1944. Before being deported to Auschwitz, Jews from the Theresienstadt ghetto were made to appear in a Nazi propaganda film, which was to be shown in Germany. It showed them sitting by a swimming pool, reading in the library, working as tailors and shoe repairers and even at a tea dance. Children were seen to be playing happily and a canteen, where plenty of food was on display, had also been scripted into the film. Other scenes in the film showed German soldiers - the comments made were on the lines of 'the Jews are enjoying good living, whilst the German soldiers are suffering death and hardship in order to safeguard the Fatherland.'

The scriptwriter and director appointed by the Nazis died in Auschwitz in November 1944. Very few of the Jews who took part in the film survived.

On 7th October 1944, 450 Jews who were made to take the corpses from the gas chambers to the furnaces, revolted. They blew up one of the four gas chambers, this with explosives which had been smuggled to them by Jewish women who were working in the Union armaments factory.

As they tried to escape from the camp, they were shot.

The women who had passed the explosives from the factory were arrested. They were tortured but did not betray anyone. They were hanged three months later.

On 13th October 1944, Antwerp was hit by a German V2 rocket - thirty-two civilians died. On that same day, in the afternoon, a VI flying bomb hit the slaughterhouse. Civilians and butchers were killed. The offensive had started.

On 1st November 1944, British and Canadian troops crossed the river Scheldt, in order to open Antwerp to the Allied military transports. By the end of November, the Allied convoy of ships reached the port.

On 10th November, an American officer, Brigadier General Clare Armstrong reached Antwerp. He set up an Anti-Flying Bomb Command, which consisted of six hundred anti-aircraft guns and communication system, which would detect the flying bombs and shoot them down before they could reach Antwerp. Thirty two of the defenders of Antwerp were killed.

There was, however, no defence against the faster-than-sound V2 rocket.

On 10th November 1944, a Belgian collaborator, Fernand Daumeries, who had helped the Nazis with great zeal, was brought to trial. He was sentenced to death for inhumane behaviour at the Breendonk camp, set up near Antwerp.

Winter 1944 was, indeed, a sad period for the port of Antwerp. 3,752 Belgian civilians lost their lives as V2 rockets hit the port. Moreover, 731 Allied servicemen were also killed by the rockets which fell on Antwerp.

On 22nd December 1944, the German offensive in the Ardennes proved to be successful. Notwithstanding this, Field Marshall von Runstedt wanted Hitler to authorise a withdrawal to the Eifel Mountains. The Führer refused.

Meanwhile, when the Germans called upon Major-General Anthony McAuliffe, the American commander beleaguered in Bastogne, to surrender, the American's answer was simply, "Nuts!", an excellent American expression, which was translated for the Nazis into the English equivalent: "Go to hell!"

When the fog cleared, the Allies' air superiority was secured and Bastogne could be supplied by air. By Christmas Eve, the Nazi offensive towards Antwerp had been stopped.

On 1st January 1945, at some time after midnight, another Nazi flying bomb fell on Antwerp. Thirty seven civilians were killed.

Throughout France, Belgium and Western Holland, almost a thousand German fighters attacked Allied airfields. This was the planned attack by the Germans when the Ardennes offensive started but which had been postponed because of fog.

On 14th January 1945, the Americans freed their trapped comrades-in-arms at Bastogne. The Germans were now in a hopeless situation.

On 8th February 1945, Canadian forces initiated Operation Veritable - this was to capture the area between the river Maas and the river Rhine.

General de Lattre de Tassigny's Operation Cheerful was against the Germans trapped at Colmar. The battle lasted twenty days; 1,600 French and 540 American soldiers lost their lives. At the end of the battle, the Germans pulled back across the Upper Rhine. 22,000 German soldiers were taken prisoner.

On 27th March, the Germans launched the last V2 rockets. This was done from their one remaining site near The Hague. One rocket fell on London at 7 a.m., killing 134 people in a block of flats in Stepney; the other came down in Antwerp and killed 27 people. That same afternoon, the third rocket fell in Orpington, Kent, and killed a civilian.

In England, 2,855 had been killed. In Belgium, 4,483 people were killed by this weapon.

Shortages of food were causing starvation to German-occupied Holland. On 29th April 1945, a mercy operation took place from the air. Three thousand British bombers parachuted more than six thousand tons of supplies to the Dutch behind German lines in Rotterdam and The Hague. It was called

Operation Manna - one could say an appropriate name relating back to biblical times when food was miraculously provided for the Israelites in the wilderness during their flight from Egypt.

On 5th May 1945, the German forces surrendered in Holland at Wageningen. At 4 p.m., in the presence of a Canadian officer, Lieutenant General Charles Foulkes, and Prince Bernhard of the Netherlands, the surrender was signed. General Blaskowitz, the Commander of German forces in Holland, was most submissive when he met the Prince. The latter just ignored the German.

It should be remembered that Prince Bernhard, born a German, had become a Dutch national and his conduct during the war years had been exemplary - he had behaved like a true Dutchman.

On 7th May 1945, at Reims, at 1.41 in the morning, General Jodl signed the final and complete surrender of all German forces on all fronts. The signing was attended by General Ivan Susloparov of Russia and General François Sevez of France. General Bedell Smith signed for the Allied Expeditionary Force, General Susloparov for the Soviet High Command and General Sevez signed as a witness. This surrender was to come into force at fifty nine minutes to midnight. A further signing took place in Berlin on 8th May 1945 - after the Reims surrender.

In Paris, Pierre Laval, who had been premier of the Vichy government in 1942 and had collaborated with the Germans, was found guilty of treason. He tried to commit suicide in October 1945 but did not succeed. He was shot by a French firing squad on 15th October 1945.

In Lille, in 1946, Jacques Desoubrie, who had betrayed his countrymen to the Gestapo in 1943, was hanged.

On 7th May 1946, the founder of the Dutch National Socialist Movement, Anton Mussert, an eager supporter of the Nazis in Holland, was hanged in The Hague.

On 7th April 1947, Rudolf Hoess, the former Commandant at Auschwitz, where he had lived with his wife and five children, was hanged for his crimes against humanity.

In Belgium, on 12th April 1947, sixteen Belgians, who had tortured prisoners incarcerated at the Breendonk camp, near Antwerp, were executed by being shot in the back.

The coffins of 6,300 American war dead, who had graves in France, were shipped back to New York on 25th October 1947. A few days later, several thousand more coffins left Antwerp for the United States.

General Blaskowitz, Commander of the German forces in Holland, committed suicide in his prison cell on 5th February 1948.

The Military Governor of Paris, Otto von Stuelpnagel, committed suicide before his trial.

Joseph Kieffer, second in command at Gestapo headquarters in Paris in 1943 and 1944, was found guilty of executing British paratroopers in Normandy in 1944. Kieffer was also responsible for sending Noor Inayat Khan, an Indian princess and direct descendant of Tipoo Sultan, to her death. Being bilingual in French and English, she worked as a British agent in France. She was sent to Dachau, where she was shot.

General Alexander von Falkenhausen, the German Military Governor in Brussels, who ordered the execution of several hundred Belgian hostages and the deportation of 25,000 Belgian Jews to Auschwitz, was sentenced to twelve years' imprisonment. In July 1944, he had been imprisoned by Hitler for having been too lenient. Moreover, he had also sympathised with those who had organised the July Plot against Hitler. The Belgians released him in April 1951.

On 9th October 1954, SS Colonel Helmut Knochen, who in 1940 had headed the Paris Gestapo, was found guilty and sentenced to death. Three and half years later, this sentence was reduced to forced labour for life. A year and half after that, the sentence was reduced to twenty years' penal servitude. Finally, he was released and went home to Baden Baden.

In 1940, Jean Moulin stayed at his post, as prefect of Chartres. He tried to help his people. When he was arrested, and told to sign a convention which blamed French soldiers for atrocities committed by the Germans, he refused. He was tortured and attempted to commit suicide by cutting his own throat. He was sent to hospital where he recovered. He was dropped from the civil service by Vichy.

It took him more than a year to reach London. Three months later, he was back in France as Délégué Général for General De Gaulle. Although he had recovered from his throat wound, his voice was hoarse and he always wore a scarf to cover his scarred throat.

He was asked by De Gaulle to co-ordinate the groups, as many leaders of the Resistance had been captured or broken off contact with London.

On 19th December 1964, the remains of Jean Moulin, a national hero, were interred in the Panthéon in Paris.

We are now in 1998. Millions of people died during the Second World War. Have any lessons been learned?